Don't Be Stingy with *Your* Prayers

Chaplain Tom Conti

Published by Faithful Life Publishers
North Fort Myers, FL 33903
FaithfulLifePublishers.com
info@flpublishers.com

Published in the United States of America

23 22 21 20 19   1 2 3 4 5

DEDICATION

This book, dedicated to my mother, Kathryn Conti, who always encouraged me to pray. She prayed me through Vietnam. She was the inspiration for, *Don't Be Stingy with Your Prayers.*

FOREWORD

Prayer we all need to pray more and we need more people to pray for us, God can help us do this.

1 Thessalonians 5:17, "pray without ceasing." This seems to be an impossible task when you are trying to go from little or no prayer to praying all the time. We need to start small and end up big. How do you eat an elephant? One bite at a time.

2 Corinthians 9:6, "But this I say, he who soweth sparingly shall reap sparingly, but he who soweth bountifully shall reap bountifully."

We all want bountiful, we must build up to it. Ask God to get you started and keep you going. He is eagerly waiting for your prayers.

Ephesians 2:10, "We are His workmanship created in Christ Jesus unto good works, which God had preordained so we shall walk in them."

"We are what we repeatedly do. Excellence then is not an act but a habit." Aristotle

I pray that you will be superabundantly blessed!

Ephesians 3:20, "Now unto him that is able to do exceeding abundantly above all that we ask or think according to the power that works in us."

In Jesus Precious Holy Name, I pray with thanksgiving!

Amen,

Tom Conti

ACKNOWLEDGEMENTS

I would like to thank Joy Rocco and James Wendorf for formatting the book for publishing. Thanks also to my wife, Janet Conti, for her editing. I thank God for His help and inspiration and giving me the ability to write this book.

TABLE OF CONTENTS

SALVATION

DO YOU KNOW WHERE YOU ARE GOING?

This is a simple question. Do you know if you are going to heaven? Most people will say yes I am going to heaven. Are you sure? The other place, we do not like to mention hell, is real.

Romans 10:9, "That if you shall confess with your mouth that Jesus is Lord of your life, and believe in your heart that God raised Him from the dead, than you are saved." This is a simple guarantee of salvation.

We are all sinners. Romans 3:23, "For all have sinned and come short of the glory of God."

The only person without sin was Jesus Christ. There for we all need to repent, be sorry for our sins.

2 Peter 3:9, "The Lord is not slack concerning His promise, as some men count slackness, but is longsuffering towards us-ward, not willing that any should perish, but that all should come to repentance."

You can pray these scriptures for those you want saved. I pray for several daily. It is hard to minister to your family. Jesus could not minister in Nazareth. His half-brother James was not a believer until He saw Jesus raised from the dead.

The average Christian leads one person in his lifetime to salvation. Sad? Well what about Billy Graham and all those big time Evangelists that lead, have lead great multitudes? It seems to balance out the equation somehow.

I encourage you to share this book with others.

I challenge you to expand your prayer life. "DO NOT BE STINGY WITH YOUR PRAYERS!"

May God bless you and your families superabundantly?

Ephesians 3:20, "Now unto him that is able to do exceeding abundantly , superabundantly, above all that we ask or think, according to the power that works in us."

Remember to pray like your life and the lives of those you pray for depend on it because it does.

In the precious Holy Name of Jesus, we pray thanksgiving and praise!

Amen,

Tom

INTRODUCTION

Stingy is a word we do not hear too much today. Webster and other sources define stingy as "scanty, cheap, chintzy, closefisted, mean, mangy, miserly, parsimonious, or penny-pinching. Do you get the meaning? Do any of these descriptive adjectives perhaps apply to someone you know?

In the story, the Christmas Carol, Ebenezer Scrooge is the classic example of being very stingy. His description is as a heartless miser.

I pray for many people. I have also heard many people pray.

The following may be familiar to you: I pray for my wife, my son, his wife and me. Us 4 and no more. Or, my name is Jimmy, I will take all you gimme. As selfish as these sound, surely there are many other prayers prayed in a similar manner.

Is it bette to be stingy than not to pray at all? I would say, yes! Any prayer is better than no prayer at all and we should never let a day go by without praying.

I attended Catholic school where I prayed a lot. We prayed many "Our Fathers and Hail Marys" and the rosary. At bedtime, I would ask God to bless all my family and friends, naming them all.

After graduating, I cut back on praying and stopped going to church. There are seasons for everything as it says in Ecclesiastes 3:3, *"to everything there is a season, and a time to every purpose unto heaven."* This was my season of pulling away and questioning, however, the older I get, the more I do pray. I challenge everyone reading this to expand your prayer life, and get closer to God.

The bible instructs us to pray as in 1 Thessalonians 5:17, *"Pray without ceasing…"*

At first, this can be difficult. To go from a place of not praying at all to pray all the time is where you ultimately want to be. Start slowly and gradually increase the time spent in prayer. Soon prayer will become part of what you do, and feel comfortable and right.

When we pray, we talk to God and He will always listen. When we read the bible, God will talk to us through the scriptures! It's that simple.

The following is a true story concerning a young, single mom:

She received a call at work that her daughter had broken her arm playing in the schoolyard. She ran to the hospital to find out her daughter-needed surgery. Her insurance would not cover it. She was barely making ends meet and now was losing money for lost time at work while spending time at the hospital. That night, she pulled into her driveway and started to cry. Then she cursed God, blaming Him for all of this. As she sat in her car, God spoke to her. He said, "My child, I have been waiting to hear from you and I am so glad you finally spoke to me." *WOW!* Do you know the kind of God we have? He will be happy to hear from us whatever the situation. The rest of the story? The mom started praying and going to church! She then met a Christian man, married him and lived happily ever after. Praise God! We give Him all the glory!

Do not be like the single mom, waiting for trouble before praying. Start now. Just simply pray: "Father God, it's me (your name). Please help me through another day, in Jesus

Name I pray, amen. "This will be repeated as many times as it needs to be.

When you pray, you are not always aware of the effectiveness of your prayers. It may seem as though nothing has changed, but we aren't aware of what is happening in the spiritual realm. God hears all prayers. The answers may not always be what you want or expected, but answers will come. Prayer does work for the good. Blessings will be yours because of your prayers, all you need to do is ask.

2 Corinthians 9:6 (NKJ), "He who sows sparingly shall reap sparingly and he who sows bountifully shall reap bountifully." This is an unfailing law taught by Jesus. In other words, you get what you give. This is a promise from God and one He will reward us accordingly.

Why am I writing this book? The Holy Spirit has inspired me to share with you twenty plus years of intercessory prayer and related ministry experience. My hope is that this book will give you a new outlook on prayer, fanning the spark God has put in you to be the person of prayer He has created you to be.

My mother, Kathryn, went home to the Lord April 4th, 1991. She was 83. I will never forget her last words spoken to me. She had a stroke, which was draining her life from her and altered her voice to a deep, raspy tone. My wife and I had just told her we would pray for her and her response in that unfamiliar tone was "don't be stingy with your prayers." This really rattled me, literally sending a chill down my spine. She died a few hours later.

Mom was a praying person, having had a strict Catholic upbringing and education. The nuns taught her well. She graduated St James High School in Newark, NJ. She prayed for both her sons serving in the armed forces, my brother, Jerry, who served in Korea and myself, served in Vietnam. She prayed us through many tests and trials that may have turned out much differently if not for those prayers!

Who is praying for you right now? Whom would you want to be praying for you? Most families have a person or persons who "prayer people" are usually being a mother or grandmother. If you don't have one in your family, perhaps you can become one! For a season, my mother-in-law became the prayer person my wife and I relied on to pray for us. Then God showed us Jeremiah 29:11 and the plan He ordained for us. We became Born Again Christian Believers in 1995 and my wife, Janet, and I then began working as a prayer team and continue to do so. I was asked to be Chaplain for the Veterans group I belonged to and began the process of being credentialed to be an ordained Minister of the Gospel of our Lord and Savior, Jesus Christ. We created the VIP (Veterans' Intercessory Prayer) team at the same time. This is an internet team of Christians, joined in prayer for thousands of requests. It began about 10 years ago with 2 of us and has grown to 60 in 16 states and overseas. We have about 30 pastors on the team whose congregations also will pray. The team represents all arms of the military as well as all wars concerned. We pray daily for each other as well as honoring others' requests.

My wife and I are also altar prayer workers at our church, do hospital visitation and head 2 ministries, one for the homeless, Feed MY Sheep, and another that I do for the veterans.

Our life is a constant flow of prayer and intercession. However, it wasn't always the case—it took God's calling and our obedient following, putting down the past and taking our position in His will. In addition, it's been such a rewarding life!

Men need to pray. At most, of the prayer meetings I have attended, you can count the men on one hand. Someone once said men don't eat quiche, ask for directions or pray? I am praying for you to expand your prayer life. This book can help you. If you knew the blessings you, your family, and loved ones are missing because of lack of prayer, you would be on your knees 24/7. The shortest distance between a problem and a solution is between the floor and your knees. Our key scripture is paraphrased in you reap what you sow or get what you give. Do unto others what you would have them do unto you. You need to understand the relevance of this. Praying is not an option; it is a requirement to a blessed, fulfilled life in Jesus. The bible tells us to pray without ceasing, pray daily and read the Word! The Word is life. All your answers to everything you want to know are in the bible. God speaks to you through scripture. Every case of backsliding, falling away from God, can be traced to having stopped praying and reading the bible. The enemy of your soul will try every way he can to stop your prayers and stop you from reading the Word. He will use every distraction to do this.

Does someone in your family or you need a healing, financial blessing, job, better relationships or something else? All this comes from God—ask Him in prayer. Pray from your heart as little children pray, expecting to receive. Mark 11:22-26. God loves you and He wants to help you, but you must ask Him.

Father, in Jesus' name I pray for those who read this book. Give them wisdom and knowledge as it says in James 1:5 (NIV), "If any of you lacks wisdom, he should ask God, who gives generously to all without finding fault and it will be given to him." Bless these readers superabundantly, more than they could ask or need. (Eph 3:20) Give them the ability to continue to move forward in their prayer life.

> In Jesus' name,
> I pray with thanksgiving,
>
> Amen

PRAYERS BEFORE PRAYING

"What peace we often forfeit, what needless pain we bear, all because we do not bring everything to God in prayer:" Joseph Scriver, 1855 hymn: "What a Friend We Have in Jesus."

Lord, I have no merit of my own on which to base any answer to prayer. I throw myself on your mercy—without you, I am nothing.

I believe you have worked for me, Lord. In humble faith, I take my seat in heavenly places in Christ Jesus. Ephesians 2:6

Teach me how to fulfill this sacred ministry, Lord, how to exercise the authority, which you have entrusted to me. Train me day by day that I may attain the full stature of the perfect man in Christ so that in me, your purpose of the ages may be fulfilled. Ephesians 2:7

Prayer is not only asking, but an attitude of the mind producing an atmosphere in which asking is natural.

Prayer is Power: we as Christians do not truly know the *power* our prayers generate. Our Lord and Savior, Jesus Christ's atonement for our sins empowers us with His righteousness in order for us to face the spiritual battles we are facing in the evil filled world in which we live.

We need to pray as though our lives and those of others depend on it—as they do!

DAILY PRAYER TO THE HOLY SPIRIT

Blessed Holy Spirit of God, please help me today not to grieve you. Holy Spirit you are my helper. I need you. Will you help me now?

THE BLOOD COVENANT

Father, I am so thankful for the redemption and the redemptive blood of Christ. I plead the blood of Jesus Christ and declare that the blood of Jesus Christ covers me, my family, my ministry, business, job and anything I have anything to do with, known or unknown to me, in the spirit realm and the natural realm, through the blood covenant I have with you. Father, through Jesus Christ, I declare today will be the most fruitful and glorious day of my life as I work and walk together with you. Amen. So be it.

PRAY WITHOUT CEASING

1 Thessalonians 5:17, "…Pray without ceasing." This is a command from God along with others in Chapter 5 of First Thessalonians.

Luke 18:1, "And He spoke a parable to them to this end that men ought always to pray and not faint." (Meaning not to lose heart.)

I have heard of "prayer warrior church ladies" who pray every hour they are awake. Impressive! We are not liable to do that. The closest we can get is to pray in between the other things we do.

Smith Wigglesworth was a praying man. He was (and is) a hard act to follow. I have read several of his books and those written by his sons and grandsons. During an interview, he was asked the question, how long do you pray? His response was, "I pray for about 5 minutes." Knowing he was a powerful man of prayer, the interviewer was shocked. Smith then went on to explain: "Yes, I pray for five minutes, then I go about what I was doing for five minutes, then I pray again for five minutes…" So, every hour he was awake, he prayed for thirty minutes! Wow! That sure is a hard act to follow!

Can you pray when in line at the market? Stopped at a red light? Whenever the time is available? Yes, you *can* pray without ceasing. When driving, I look for people to pray for. It is easy to pray for a person on crutches, as they need healing for their leg, or whatever is the cause for the crutches. However, what if they were not on crutches? Sure, everyone has needs, but who knows what they are? The Holy Spirit does. This would be where praying in tongues comes in. We often do not know how to pray but God does. Romans 8:26 "Likewise the Spirit also helps our infirmities, for we know not what we should pray for as we ought, but the Spirit itself makes intercession for us, with groaning which cannot be uttered."

If you do not have the gift of tongues, you need to pray for it. Get serious about receiving it. It will help you beyond anything you can imagine. Ultimately for God's Glory is the main reason for receiving the baptism of the Holy Spirit.

Luke 18:1, tells us not to lose heart. Do not give into doubt, fear, unbelief or discouragement or use excuses for unbelief when prayer you do not receive an immediate answer. Rebuke and resist all opposition to the answer and all suggestions of failure. These come from the enemy of your soul. It is a divine, blood bought right to get an answer from God, so do not lose heart.

Luke tells us about the unjust judge. He got so weary of the widow's persistent demands he finally granted her what she wanted. We could say, the squeaky wheel gets the oil!

Daniel prayed for 21 days and ate no pleasant food. The Daniel fast was then established. Chapter 10 in the book of Daniel tells us of the spiritual warfare going down at that time.

Ephesians 6:12, "For we wrestle not against flesh and blood, but against principalities, against powers, against the rulers of darkness of this world, against spiritual wickedness in high places."

The enemy does not want you to pray at all. The thought of you praying without ceasing puts you on the next level.

Pray now, Father God, I thank you for helping me to expand my prayer life. I pray that I will never be stingy with my prayers.

Ephesians 3:20, "Now unto him that is able to do exceedingly above all that we ask or think according to the power that works in us." (God's Holy Spirit.)

In Jesus' name, I pray. Amen.

WHAT TO PRAY FOR

There is no shortage of things for which to pray. You may think you do not need a list, but I have learned, as a teacher, do not take anything for granted.

1. Pray for yourself. Several students I pray for do not pray for themselves. You cannot build a house without a good foundation. Think of the first building block as prayers for yourself. Keep it simple: Father God, it is I, (your name). Thank you for getting me through another day, and for all my tomorrows. Amen. Use scripture if you like. Favorites are Psalms 23 and 91.

2. Pray to receive the Holy Spirit. There are scriptures that cover this in detail. The baptism of the Holy Spirit is a gift from God. You may think you do not need this gift, but once you receive it, you will be amazed how you existed without it!

3. Pray: God have mercy on me, a sinner. Luke 18:13 and Psalm 67:1. We are *all* sinners (saved by Grace) and fall short. Ask God to help you to not sin.

4. Pray for our enemies. Matthew 5:44, Jesus tells us to do this. It is a difficult thing to do. It takes time and practice. Only God's Grace can give you the power to pray for those who hurt you. Luke 23:32, "Father, forgive them for they know not what they do." These were Jesus' words while on the cross.

5. Pray for your family, salvation for the unsaved, deliverances (from addictions and things tormenting others), healings, which can also include broken relationships and mending broken bridges. Life is too short to have severed ties with family.

6. Pray for all unsaved—yes, we want to evangelize the world. Luke 10:2, "Pray for the Lord of the harvest to send laborers into His harvest."

7. Pray for all pastors and their families. All five-fold Ministers, Apostles, Prophets, Evangelists, Pastors and Teachers. Ephesians 4:11.

8. Pray for our leaders (whether you like them or not). 1 Timothy 2:2, "Pray for all Kings and all who are in authority that we may lead a quiet and peaceful life in all goodness and reverence.

9. Pray God heals the sick. James 5:16, "Confess your faults to one another, and pray for one another that ye may be healed. The effectual fervent prayer of a righteous man availeth much." (KJV)

10. Pray for the United States of America, one nation under God. Put God back in our schools, courts, work places, churches and our lives.

11. Pray for our troops—in this country and around the world. Psalm 91—that God would give His angels charge over them in all their ways.

12. Pray for our first responders: police, firefighters, EMTs etc.

13. Pray for banning of abortion!

This is a short list. What are the important things for which you feel urged to pray?

WHAT A FRIEND I HAVE IN JESUS
Joseph Schiven 1855

What a friend I have in Jesus
All my sins and grief to bear
What a privilege to carry
Everything to God in prayer!

Oh what peace I often forfeit
Oh what needless pain I bear
All because I do not carry
Everything to God in prayer!

Have I trials and temptations?
Is there trouble anywhere?
I should never be discouraged
I take it to the Lord in prayer.

Can I find a friend so faithful
Who will all my sorrows share?
Jesus knows my every weakness
I take it to the Lord in prayer.

Chaplain Tom Conti

Am I weak and heavy laden
Encumbered with a load of care?
Precious Savior still my refuge
I take it to the Lord in prayer.

Do my friends despise and forsake me?
I take it to the Lord in prayer.
In His arms He will take and shield me.
I take it to the Lord in prayer.

DAILY PRAYER FOR YOUR FAMILY

I pray the blood of Jesus Christ of Nazareth over every member of my family… (Name all of them.) I bind you devil in the name of Jesus. I rebuke your spirit of fear that would cause my faith to be weak. I loose God's power; love and sound mind into my life according to 2 Timothy 1:17 and I allow His Holy Spirit to have His will in my life.

Thank you, Lord, for the armor you have given me and thank you for your Word that gives me faith, wisdom and strength.

> In Jesus's name,
> I pray with thanksgiving.
> Amen.

THANK YOU GOD

Lord, I thank you for this day. I thank you for me being able to see and hear this morning. I am blessed because you are a forgiving God and an understanding God. You have done so much for me and You keep on blessing me. Forgive me this day for everything I have done, will do, said, will say, thought or will think that was not pleasing to You. I ask now for your forgiveness. Please keep me safe from all danger and harm. Help me to start this day with a new attitude and plenty of gratitude. Let me make the best of each day and to clear my mind so I can hear from You.

Continue to use me to do Your will. Continue to bless me so I can be a blessing to others. Keep me strong so I may help the weak.

I believe that God changes people and things. I pray that all who read this will come to know there is no problem, circumstance or situation greater than God.

> This is my prayer for you.
> In Jesus's name I pray
> Amen.

PLEDGE TO THE BIBLE

"I Pledge allegiance to the Bible, God's Holy Word. I will make it a lamp unto my feet, a light unto my path and I will hide its words in my heart that I may not sin against God."

Amen.

PRAYER

"Prayer is the soul's desire, uttered or unexpressed; the motion of a hidden fire that trembles in the breast." (Montgomery)

PRAYER FOR DAILY GRACE

2 Corinthians 6:1: As God's fellow workers we urge you not to receive God's grace in vain."

Grace is the overflowing, free and unmerited favor of God, as manifested in the salvation of sinners and the bestowal of blessings. It is always available to draw from.

Prayer is the exercise of drawing on the grace of God.

PRAY NOW! DRAW ON GOD'S GRACE!

PRAYER TO OVERCOME EVIL SPIRITS

Lord, drive away all evil spirits and forbid them to have any activity in this place. Amen.

Through the blood of Jesus, I am redeemed out of the hand of the devil and all my sins are forgiven. The blood of Jesus Christ, is cleansing me from all sin. I am justified and made righteous, just as if I had never sinned. I am set apart for God. My body is a temple for the Holy Spirit, redeemed and cleansed by the blood of Jesus. I belong to Jesus now, body, soul and spirit. His blood protects me against all evil. Satan has no more power over me, no more place inside me. I renounce all evil spirits completely and declare them my enemies. Jesus said, "And these signs shall follow them that believe: In my name shall they cast out devils" Mark 16:17. I am a believer and in the name of Jesus Christ, I exercise my authority and expel all evil spirits. I command them to leave, according to the Word of God and in the name of Jesus. Amen.

WATCH AND PRAY

Oh Lord, while I am praying, I commit my duty to You and ask You to keep it from suffering any damage. I ask You to protect me for this time and forbid Satan to intrude, for I am using this time to seek your glory.

PRAYER 101

I am not going to tell you there is anything wrong with the way you are praying now. May I ask you, are your prayers being answered? Do you get discouraged and then do not pray? Are you praying regularly, daily? Do you have faith to know that you know your prayers will be answered? Have there been any miracles in your life? Do you have mountains you need to be moved? Matthew 17:20: "Truly I tell you, if you have faith as small as a mustard seed, you can say to this mountain, move from here to there, and it will move."

Would you like to answer yes to all of the above? Well, you can! As children of God, we have authority (power) through Jesus Christ, inheritance, blood covenant. All we need to do is pray according to the bible. Hosea 4:6 "My people perish for lack of knowledge." This is my quest, to show you that God loves you so much He wants to answer your prayers.

Satan, the enemy of your soul, does not want you to know this and does not want you to pray. He will distract you in every way, putting roadblocks in your path. How long can you go without breathing? One or two minutes? How long can you go without praying? Prayer is our spiritual breath. The bible tells us to pray without ceasing…1 Thes 5:17.

As Christians, we have the authority to go to the Father 24/7. He is always there and will always listen. I cannot find the words to describe to you what you are missing when you neglect to pray--- to talk to God. Blessings beyond your imagination, super abundant blessings are yours through the power of prayer. Ephesians 3:20.

Prayer should be our first response, not last resort. Don't consider prayer a religious act, but an opportunity to commune with your holy Father in heaven. It creates an atmosphere of anticipation. Mark 11:23-25. Pray--believe--receive! The bible says it, I believe it, that settles it.

Some have shared with me, they never hear from God--He never speaks to them. Have they listened? God speaks to us in many ways. Very few hear an audible voice, but many do hear that still quiet voice within the spirit. He speaks to us through scripture, others, and in dreams and visions. God wants to hear from you, and He wants to make miracles part of your life. You *have* witnessed miracles---- the moment you are born again, the birth of a baby, the act of being able to love and be loved, every new day you're alive.

Ask God to be your partner in all you do. Proverbs 16:3 "Commit to the Lord whatever you do, and your plans will succeed." James 4:2" We have not for we ask not."

When teaching, I will ask my students if they ever went to the bank to cash a check against their own account. Say you have $105.00 in your checking account.

You know you can safely cash a check for $100.00 without overdrawing your account. So you write the check and the teller hands you the money. How much do you have in your account in heaven? Can you go to God in prayer knowing in your heart He will answer?

Do you have the assurance you would never be "overdrawn" on spiritual requests?

Find some scriptures to back up your prayer requests. This is called praying by the numbers. For example, "Father God, it says in your word in 2 Peter 3:9 that you do not wish for anyone to perish, so I am standing on that word and praying for my friend, Joe, that you would put Christian believers in his path to minister to him. In Jesus's name, I pray with thanksgiving. Amen." You have just prayed a powerful prayer for Joe. Expect a praise report from Joe, that someone has crossed his path who will share the Gospel with him showing him how much God loves him.

Men have been praying for thousands of years. Do you think they would have stopped if it did not work? The bible lists many answered prayers. It is full of great stories and history. The Holy Bible is **Basic Instruction Before Leaving Earth**. Read it daily! Start in the New Testament, the Gospel of John, then Matthew, Mark and Luke. Some bibles have a plan to read them in a year. This works well. You will look forward to what the bible will reveal to you each day. You will be amazed how it will relate to what is happening in your life. Each day is like Christmas morning opening up gifts or as Forest Gump said: "….like a box of chocolates--you never know what you will get."

Another rule is, spend 30 minutes in prayer, 10 minutes reading the bible, and 10 minutes silently waiting to hear from God. Prayer is a dialogue, not a monologue. Whether you have never prayed before or have been praying for decades, you will grow in your one on one relationship with God. It is all about the relationship. James 4:8 tells us to "draw closer to God and he will draw closer to you."

We are all at different levels in our relationship with God. Different levels, different devils. We all need protection. Psalm 91 is the psalm that anticipates evil and prays protection over God's people. Ephesians 6:10-20 instructs us to put on the full armor of God. The best offense is a good defense. We live in a fallen, evil world. Pray protection over yourself before you go out in it!

LET US PRAY

This is a suggested outline to give you something to start with. We will talk about an atmosphere of prayer. You are to enter the presence of God the Father, the creator of the universe, God Almighty. The bible tells us to rise early in the morning to pray. Start with about 30 minutes. Get up early while it is quiet, Ps 63:1. A good way to begin is by reading the bible—God's Word written by man's hand.

To learn how to read the bible, you must understand it is not a novel. If you begin in Genesis, by the time you get to Numbers you most likely will be discouraged. The current, general guide is to start in the New Testament with the Gospels: Matthew, Mark, Luke and John. All have similarities although written by four different men to four different classes of people. Matthew was written to the Jews, having a Jewish emphasis. The Jews were looking for signs. Mark was written to the Romans and has an emphasis on what they were looking for, which was awards and medals. Luke was written to the Greeks. This apostle, Luke, was a doctor. The Greeks were seeking knowledge, as many were scholars. Luke was long winded and his is the longest gospel. Finally, John known as the beloved was the only disciple to die a natural death at about 100 years old. He was part of Jesus's "inner circle" with Peter and James.

Begin with the Gospel of John. Why? It is easy to understand as written to all men to give us a close account of the life of Jesus. Take your time and read it slowly. Keep a journal on your thoughts and what messages you feel God is sending you through His Word. Then proceed to the other gospels and finish reading through the New Testament.

Proverbs read one chapter daily. In one month, you will have read the entire book of Proverbs. This is part of the Old Testament.

There are many different versions of the bible. I use the New King James (NKJ), the Message and the Spirit Filled Life Bible for Students.

Many of the reference bibles are good. You can also supplement your bible reading with a devotional. I use the classic, "My Utmost for His Highest" by Oswald Chambers. This is an excellent devotional.

So now, you have read the bible for 10 minutes. God's Word tells us to …"enter His gates with thanksgiving and His courts with praise. "Ps 100:4 If you have a tape of your favorite worship music, you can begin by playing it. The Lord's Prayer (Matt 6:9-13) begins and ends with worship. Saying the Lord's Prayer is the best way to begin.

Pray, praise, repent, asks, and yield is all in the Lord's Prayer.

THE LORD'S PRAYER: (NIV)

"Our Father in heaven,
Hallowed be your name,
Your kingdom come,
Your will be done,
On earth as it is in heaven.
Give us this day our daily bread,
Forgive our debts.
As we also have forgiven our debtors,
And lead us not into temptation,
But deliver us from the evil one."

There are many people and things for prayer. Begin with yourself. Psm 91:1: "He who dwells in the shelter of the Most High will rest in the shadow of the Almighty." This prayer anticipates evil. Use it! Verse 11, "For He will command His angels concerning you to guard you in all your ways." I feel great and confident knowing I start my day under God's protection. Eph. 6:10-20 tells you to put on the full armor of God. In this evil world, we all need God's available protection to get us safely through our day.

In a later chapter, I will give you a list of things we all need to pray for, but not necessarily each day. Next, pray for your family. Prayer lists are great for writing down all close family members' names. You can then place your hand on the list and pray over them. Do this daily.

Now that you have prayed for yourself and your family, is there an upcoming event or situation you want to pray for? Now is the time. What else is on your heart for prayer?

The final one third of your allotted time with God is the most difficult. Now you must quiet your mind and wait for God to speak to you. Keep a pen handy--you may want to write down what you feel God is telling you. Remember, prayer is a dialogue not a monologue. It may take time. There can be a dry spell with no communication. Chances are someone will pop up in your mind whom you have not had contact with for years. Guess what? They need your prayers now! If you have no clue what to pray for, for that person beside the obvious salvation, deliverance, healing, prosperity etc., just ask God to bless them. If you are blessed to have the baptism of the Holy Spirit and have received your prayer language, then pray in tongues. We will cover how to receive the baptism of the Holy Spirit in a later chapter.

All done? Most important, thank Him! Mark 11:23-24. Pray, believe and receive. You have begun to move mountains. During the day, keep thanking God for all things. Prov.16:3 says to make God your partner and all your plans with succeed. Try it—it works!

Praise God!.

PRAY—PRAY—PRAY—PRAY—PRAY PRAY—PRAY—PRAY --PRAY

PRAY PERSISTENTLY: Luke:1-5

PRAY EARNESTLY: Luke 22:44

PRAY ALWAYS: Ephesians 6:18

PRAY SPECIFICALLY: Philippians 4:6, 19

PRAY FIRST THEN WORK, GOD'S ORDER: Billy Graham

PRAYER — Our first response, not last resort.

PRAYER — Life's highest privilege.

PRAYER — A hot line to God's heart.

PRAYER — A war ---- put on your armor: Ephesians 6:10-20

PRAYER — Fuel for our lives.

PRAYER — Make miracles happen: Romans 12:12.

PRAYER — Draws us closer to God: James 4:8

PRAY as though your life depends on it. It does!

PRAY as though the lives of those you pray for depends on it. It does!

PRAY without ceasing: 1 Thessalonians 5:17

PRAY—PRAY—PRAY—PRAY—PRAY

PRAY—PRAY—PRAY—PRAY

PRAYERLESSNESS

THE SOIL OF PRAYERLESSNESS PRODUCES A CROP OF DAMNATION. If you do not pray, are you going to hell? No, but prayer will certainly help keep you from going! In Galatians, Paul is blasting them for being fickle and backslidden.

Galatians 6:7-8, "***Be not deceived, God is not mocked, for whatsoever a man soweth, that shall he also reap. For he that soweth to his flesh shall of the flesh reap corruption; but he that soweth to the Spirit shall of the Spirit reap life everlasting.***" (KJ) This is a prophecy, promise and command from God.

Thursday my wife and I do a feeding for the homeless. During my prayer time, I ask God to give me a word for these people. The program is they hear the Word, we all pray the Lord's Prayer together then bless the food and eat. God has been giving me words to encourage them to pray. God knows that the Lord's Prayer, in most cases, is the only prayer these homeless folk say all week. There are 40-60 present. If the Holy Spirit convicted just one by and starts praying on a regular basis, it is a blessing. Galatians 6:7-8 was the word a few weeks ago.

It seems harsh to say that you will go to hell if you do not pray. The road to perdition and destruction is paved with prayerlessness. As a pastor and prayer councilor, every case of backsliding or falling away from God that I have encountered can be traced back to the person having stopped praying. Am I trying to scare and convict people to pray? You bet I am! Actually, I can suggest it, but God's Holy Spirit is the one who will do the convicting.

So, is it a "sin" not to pray? James 4:17, "***Therefore to him that knows to do good and does it not, to him it is a sin.***" Praying is not an option; it is our duty to God. We all know, in our hearts, we are to pray. If we do not, we commit the sin of neglecting prayer.

Say you see a baby crawling out into traffic. If you have the opportunity to go save it and you do not, is that a sin? You can answer that yourself. I pray daily for divine appointments for prayer. At times, I miss them, but I am improving and becoming more sensitive to those, God has placed in my path to minister to.

I once met a young man who had never prayed or read the bible. He has been a joy to teach, as he has no misconceptions about either one. I discovered it is easier to start with a clean slate than to try to undo wrong teaching.

The enemy will attack everyone. He does not want anyone to pray or read the bible. The last thing I want you to do is make prayer a religious act. It needs to be a spiritual conversation with God. We, as born again believers, filled with and led by the Holy Spirit. We need discipline, setting aside daily times to pray. We are not perfect. It is OK to miss one time or cut short your prayer time on rare occasions. How long can you go without breathing? Three minutes then you may die. How long can you go without prayer before you are spiritual dead? We are told to pray for our daily bread. That means it is vital to our relationship with God to stay in daily contact with Him, so He can provide us with our daily bread or whatever it is we may need.

I ask God daily to give me the words, scriptures and whatever I need to minister to those who do not understand. There is the old story about a man who gets to heaven and St. Peter shows him around. He sees a box with his name on it. He asks St Peter if he can open it and St Peter warns him against it. However, the man insists so he opens it and is overwhelmed by all the stuff in the box. St Peter then explains to the man that this is all he missed in life by not praying. "We have not because we ask not." (James 4:2)

My prayer for you to be convicted, by the Holy Spirit, to be committed to daily prayer. Prayer is our principle ministry. If we fail in prayer, we fail at everything. The most important thing you do daily is pray. It sets the stage for our day. Proverbs 16:3 "Make God you partner daily and all your plans will succeed." The highest privilege we have is praying to God and calling Him Father. He is waiting to hear from you. Start now to develop your one on one personal relationship with God. It will change your life and you will have this close relationship with Him through eternity!

In Jesus's name, we pray, Amen.

GOD LOVES YOU!

I was talking to a man raised in a mainline faith who was never told God loves him. It was not until he became a born again, spirit filled Pentecostal believer that he did learn God loves him. 1John 4:19, "We love Him (God) because He loved us first." Part of our daily prayer should always include, thank you, Father God, for loving me. It is most important that we give Him thanks everyday. John 3:16, "For God so loved the world that He gave His only begotten Son, that whosoever believe in Him should not perish but have eternal life." This is one of the most often used verses in the bible.

Just like in the old movies, during our Thursday feedings, they get to listen to the preacher first, pray and then eat. In the morning of the feeding, I ask God for a special word for His sheep, and this past week God gave me that very message--- that He loves them! Hallelujah, Praise God!

Agape love, (pronounced a-gop-pee) Webster's dictionary explains: "gaping with wonder, expectation, eager, anticipation." The agape love our heavenly Father has for us is beyond our comprehension. He loves us the same yesterday as today as He will tomorrow and forever, regardless of if we are bad or good. He created us in His image and likeness. We are His masterpiece. God does not make junk!

Some years back there was a TV program called "Touched by an Angel" which ran for a number of years. It was about angels on assignment to help those on earth experiencing problems. The favorite line was "God loves you." Some would consider this corny and unreal, but that phrase could not be truer. I really liked that show as the good guys always won and everyone lived happily ever after. Angels are real as it proclaims in Psalm 91:11, "For you shall give your angels charge over me to keep me in all my ways."

Thank you, Lord!

There are many people who have never been told they are loved, like the man I mentioned a few paragraphs ago. Do you tell your spouse, children, parents and loved ones that you love them often? Daily? Especially with the elderly, we never know when or IF we will see them again. Take a minute right now, pick up the phone (or text or email) and tell them you love them. Oh, you may say, they know I do. Not a good excuse. We know God loves us, but we also learn He wants to hear us say "thank you for loving me." God never grows weary of listening to our thanks and praise. Psalm 100:4-5: "Enter His gates with thanksgiving and enter His courts with praise; be thankful unto Him and bless His name. For the Lord is good, His mercy is everlasting and His truth endured to all generations."

Some of us get hung up and confused with the love we know of with our earthly father, and that of God Almighty. There is no comparison. Once we grasp the overwhelming reality of God's love for us we will realize how truly blessed we are. *See enclosed Father's Day message "The Field Cross."* Our earthly fathers are much harder to please than our heavenly Father is. How do we please our heavenly Father? By spending time with Him—speaking to him in prayer. "Give us this day our daily bread." This excerpt from The Lord's Prayer means that we ask God to give us, on this day, what we need. God is waiting for you, the book of James tells us if we take the first step and draw closer to God, then He will draw closer to us. It is our choice to be as close to God as we can possibly be.

Once again, the reason we were born; why we are on this earth, is to develop our one-on-one personal relationship with God.

The current economic crisis is a time of tests and trials for many. We as Christians need to declare God is on the throne; He is in charge and in control; He will never leave us or forsake us. (Duet. 31:6 and 8,; Joshua 1:5; Kings 8:57; 1 Chron 28:20 and Hebrews 13:5). Since that promise is repeated so many times in the bible, you can be absolutely certain that promise is yes and amen!" Look at the birds of the air, for they neither sow nor reap, nor gather into barns; yet your heavenly Father feeds them. Are you not of more value than they?" (Matt. 6:26). Trust God to supply all your needs. Not necessarily your "wants" but He will supply your needs. God loves you!

Father God, I thank you for loving me. I know I am not worthy but by your grace and your mercy, I am saved.

If you have never invited the Lord into your heart, say the last sentence of Luke 18:13:

"God, be merciful to me a sinner." Recite Rom 10:9, "If you shall confess with your mouth that Jesus is Lord of your life, and shall believe in your heart that God raised him from the dead, ***you shall be saved.***" (Emphasis, author). We pray this in Jesus's name.

WHY AM I HERE?

Men have pondered this thought forever....most still do not get it. Last week I went to an annual pastor's ministry meeting. These meetings are not like church on Sunday. They always carry an important message from senior ministry leaders for all to take home to their congregations. First order of business, your purpose, as a Christian, is to develop your spirituality, your walk and personal relationship with God. Wow! We all need to do this, as we need to improve our own personal relationship with the Father. How do we do this? Pray--pray--pray--pray. Get the idea? This is why we are here.

The following are six steps you can take to get to know God better:

1. Humble your spirit. 2 Chron 7:14. You are entering the throne room. Although it is open 24/7, we still need to recognize the Lord God, our heavenly Father, deserves all the humility we can give Him.

2. Be willing to please. Matt 26:41. As kids, and even as we mature, we have the desire to please our earthly dads. How much more should we please our heavenly Father? Keep His commandments and be about His business.

3. Reverential respect. Hebrews 12:28. He is God the Almighty so we have an obligation to give Him all the honor we can. We can show this honor by getting down on our knees or our faces.

4. Obedient spirit. Isaiah 1:19. When God tells us something, which we "hear" in our spirit, just DO it! Do not argue with God----that never works. God always knows best.

5. Yielding spirit. Ecc 10:4. Be led by God allowing Him to get involved in all you do and in everything in your life. We pray

about big things but the small things are just as important to God.

6.   Be eager to do His will. Ps 100. Thank Him continually. We should be as excited today about pleasing Him as we were the day we were saved.

The greatest privilege we have as Christians is to call God "Father" in our prayers. Luke 11:2-4.

Recently, I spent some time with a man who never opened a bible or prayed. This is hard for most of us to understand, but people like him are out there. It will be much easier for this man to learn for he has no preconceptions. I am anxious to witness his growth in the Word.

What does God have to do to get your attention? Just about every testimony I have heard is based on the deepest valley a person can get into and not have any hope of climbing out without God.

We are all on different levels with our intimate, personal relationships with God, and we do have an adversary fighting against us. There is a saying: "Different levels, different devils" meaning as you mature in your spirituality, your challenges will be greater. We are all perpetually under attack from an invisible enemy of our soul, who does not want us to develop a relationship with God. But the Lord instructs us not to fear ---- God is our shield and strong tower. He is always with us. "Greater is He that is in us, than he that is in the world." 1 John 4:4. The best offense is a good defense: put on God's armor daily! Ehp. 6:10-20.

In my yearly meeting, which I must attend as a requirement for my licensing to maintain my ordination, I am blessed to be in the company of men holding all the offices the bible speaks of: apostles, prophets, evangelists, pastors and teachers. (Eph. 4:11). The general attendance is mostly comprised of pastors. I look forward to this meeting and I have signed up many intercessors to participate on my VIP (Veterans Intercessory Prayer) Team. I have also made new friends. This is not the kind of meeting which focuses mainly on praise and worship and comfortable teaching. It is the fire and brimstone teaching that is difficult to both present and hear, but very necessary, as it reminds us of our mortality and of our obligation of obedience to our Lord. We are here because of His purpose, not our own!

The first topic at these meetings is usually: "*What Have You Done to Improve Your Personal Relationship with God?*" This is a question every Christian needs to address. How would you answer? Have you prayed more or spent more time reading the bible? It is no secret the primary reason for backsliding and pulling away from God is lack of both these activities.

Every Tuesday morning, I teach at Teen Challenge in Ft Myers, Florida. When I arrive on campus, if I notice travel bags stacked by the office I know someone is leaving for the wrong reasons. I will always ask if I may speak to and pray with the departing student. My first question: "When did you stop praying and/or reading your bible?" The student is usually unsettled that I know he indeed did stop these practices, and curious as to how I knew! My response is he wouldn't be leaving if he were still praying and reading his bible. Some will confess it has been days. More than one day gives the enemy the open door to attack as the armor has fallen and left the individual vulnerable. We all need to put on the full armor of God daily (Eph 6:11-18 KJV), "Put on the whole armor of God, that you may be able to stand against the wiles of the devil." The child of God, covered by the sacred blood of Jesus, has the authority to rebuke the enemy. Stand strong in prayer and the Word daily!

How long should we pray? There is no obligation only the desire to spend as much time as you can with the Lord. Sometimes there is very little time, and short prayers are meaningful too. You don't have to pray and read for hours and hours every day. That is just not feasible. But do your best and as you continue on your personal journey, you will find you really enjoy and look forward to those times in prayer and studying the Word. The Lord's Prayer is always a good place to begin.

If you have never read the bible, start in the Gospels: Matthew, Mark, Luke and John. I would suggest beginning with John. Although John is the last gospel written, it is the easiest to understand and it is a beautiful book of enlightenment and joy. John was said to be the favorite disciple of Jesus.

God loves you --- He longs for fellowship with you. He is patient, but will sometimes do the unexpected to gain your attention. The wonderful evangelist, Billy Graham, is quoted as saying: *"When we pray, God goes to work."*

The prayer of Jabez in 1 Chron. 4:10, "Jabez cried out to the God of Israel "Oh that you would bless me and enlarge my territory! Let your hand be with me, and keep me from evil so that I will be free from pain." And God granted his request.

Although God already knows your heart and your need, He wants to hear from you --- He wants you to ask Him for help because He knows you do need His strength.

My prayer for you is to expand and develop your relationship with God.

In Jesus's name, I pray.

GROW IN GRACE, KNOWLEDGE AND FAITH

2 Peter 3:18, "but grow in grace and in the knowledge of our Lord and Savior Jesus Christ. To Him be glory both now and forever. Amen." This is a command from God. The Christian life is growth. Every grace and blessing of the gospel is in seed form and implanted in the newly Born Again child of God. 1 Peter 1:23 and James 1:18. These seeds will grow to full maturity if are watered from heaven and cared for by the individual in conformity to the Word of God, No one, or a dozen works or an anointing of the Holy Spirit will make a person fully mature and beyond the growing stage of Christian experience. One must walk in the light as he receives knowledge and he will grow to maturity in Christ. 1 John 1:17 and 1 Peter 2:1-8.

Years back when I was newly born again, I thought, that was it — I could sit back and relax. I did not get it. A new world of spiritual opportunities was unfolding before me, and my calling then was to embrace this infilling of the Holy Spirit and do my part to saturate my mind with His Word and pray for guidance in my learning, embracing the information I would receive from the bible and teachers God was placing in my path.

EIGHTEEN DEFINITIONS OF FAITH

1.	Substance of things hoped for	Heb 11:1
2.	Evidence of things not seen	Heb 11:1, 7
3.	Invisible backing of elders	Heb 11:2
4.	Creative power of divine works	Heb 11:3
5.	Divine testimony of right doing	Heb 11:4
6.	Cancellation of natural laws	Heb 11:5
7.	Basis of pleasing God	Heb 11:6
8.	Dependence upon God's Word	Heb 11:7
9.	Trust in the unknown future	Heb 11:8-10
10.	Counting things that be not as though they were	Heb 11:11 and Romans 4:17
11.	Seeing invisible things	Heb 11:13-16
12.	Assurance of God's faithfulness	Heb 11:17-19, 10:23
13.	Confidence of things to come	Heb 11:20-31, Ephesians 3:12 and 1 John 3:21
14.	Stimulus of Christianity	Heb 11:32, 12:2
15.	The life blood of the just	Heb 10:38
16.	Shield of Christian armor	Eph 6:16
17.	Down payment of things desired 10:23, and 35-39.	Heb 3:6, 12:14, 6:11-12,
18.	Guarantee of Answered Prayer 24, Heb 11:6	Matt 21:22, Mark 11:22-

As small children there is a season when we discover the more we know the more is expected of us. The parable of the talents teaches to he who is given much, much is required. With athletes, when a level of performance is achieved, it is expected to be maintained.

I have worked with new believers who are hungry to learn everything. I had and have to be careful not to overwhelm them. Slow and steady gets the job done. It takes time --- it is a growing "process" and we all are different. Some say three years is a good point to check your development. This is done by knowing where you were, spiritually, when your journey began and where you are now. When are we done? Never! I know mighty men of God who have been pastors for 50 years and are still learning. Look at Billy Graham who is over 90 years old. His life has been such a tremendous inspiration to countless people, including United States Presidents, and he continues to grow. My wife and I saw the movie, "Billy, the Early Years." Like any of us, he did not wake up one day and decide to be an Evangelist. It was a process for him too and at one point even, he was challenged on his beliefs, which led him to discover how important faith is.

Hebrews 11 is the faith chapter. Read it. Total trust in God with no doubts — that is faith. Hebrews 11:1, "Now Faith is the substance of things hoped for, the evidence of things not seen."

The word faith is used 24 times in Hebrews 11 and 458 times in the bible (NIV). The mighty men of God listed in Chapter 11 are the faith heroes' hall of fame.

SALVATION AND HEALING

3 John 2, "Beloved, I wish above all things that you may prosper and be in health, even as your soul prospers." There are three blessings in this verse. Material prosperity, bodily healing and health and soul salvation. What more can we ask?

At some point in our Christian walk, we get the salvation message. It is hard to wrap our minds around it: Jesus died for us, all those many years ago. He died so we can live. This is our salvation! Even though we were not born yet, He died for our sins past, present and future. This is an absolute fact we, at some point, must accept, but stop before we receive the rest. Salvation in the Greek means healing. This is even more difficult to grasp. Isaiah 53:5, "by His stripes, (Jesus's) we ARE healed." It is already done. Jesus proclaimed on the cross while He was dying: "It is finished." Thank you, Jesus!

There are 35 facts related to sickness and healing backed by over 220 scriptures in the bible. OK, so why so many Christians are sick, poor and missing God's blessings. Hosea 4:6, "My people perish for lack of knowledge." You must read the Word, know what the bible teaches, and believe it. Why do we doubt God's Word? We need to become as little children again taking the bible as God's spoken word written by man's hand. Let your creed be: God said it, I believe it that settles it.

I use a 12-part teaching on Divine Health and Healing. God does not want us to be sick. This is not His will. How can we be about His business if we are sick? Pray for help, His grace, mercy and healing. God always hears your prayers---not your silence.

To remain in line with God's will, pray every day and read your bible. All you need to know is in those pages. God's Word is alive ---- it gives life, healing, comfort and joy.

We are all at different spiritual levels and God will meet you where you are to bring you to where He wants you to be. We all need a personal relationship with God. This is the foundation of a blessed life.

The Lord's Prayer has all we need to get started. Say it slowly and pay attention to what you're praying. "Give us this day our daily bread…" This means supply our needs --- not necessarily our "wants." Be careful what you pray for as you are then responsible for what you ask for. Pray for HIS will in your life. Come before the Lord with a spirit of thanksgiving. Humble yourself and be grateful. He is a good God and He knows your needs better than even you do! Develop an attitude of gratitude. James 4:8, "Draw close to God and He will draw close to you." He loves fellowship with you. That's why He created mankind!

Again, it is so important that you "Do not be stingy with your prayers." All of our prayers are saved and stored in heaven! You reap what you sow: no prayer, no power; some prayer, some power; many prayers, much power. Look for reasons to pray, not excuses not to. Do not miss the blessings you would receive through prayer! This is for your benefit ---- God wants to hear from you so He can bless you. He is a very good listener!

When I have really transacted business with God on His covenant and let go entirely, there is no sense of merit, no human ingredient in it, but a complete overwhelming sense of being brought into union with God. The entire experience is transfigured with peace and joy. Amen!

Until we develop, heighten and increase our personal relationship with God, we will not enjoy all the blessings He has in store for us. We need to commune with Him daily and read His Word so it saturates our heart. We need to hunger for time with Him and wait for His Holy Spirit's guidance in every choice and decision, and we need to recognize what a privilege and an honor it is to truly be a child of the living God!

The following is a powerful prayer. Use it often, even daily. We as God's chosen, His children have the authority of the blood covenant we have with the Father.

"Father, I am so thankful for the redemption and the redemptive blood of Jesus Christ. I plead the blood of Jesus Christ and declare the blood covers me, my family, my ministry, business, job and anything I have anything to do with, known or unknown to me, in the spirit and natural realm, through the blood covenant I have with You, Father, through Jesus Christ.

I declare today will be the most fruitful and glorious day of my life as I work and walk together with You, Lord. Amen.

COVENANT

Webster says: "covenant: an agreement or stipulation; the promises of God as revealed in scriptures; the solemn compact between members of a church to maintain it's faith, discipline etc. In law, an undertaking or promise of legal validity."

How many times is covenant used in the Bible? There is no single correct way to translate the ancient Hebrew, Aramaic and Greek Bible manuscripts into English. The grammar, structure and style of those languages are very different from English, and a literal word-for-word translation is not possible. Therefore, the number of times a particular word appears is usually different for each version of the Bible. Covenant appears varying from 272 to 313 times, depending on the version. It is safe to say covenant is used frequently in God's Word, although it is not in popular use today. It is a legal, binding term that cannot be broken. A blood covenant is literally sealed in blood.

Some examples are:

Genesis 9:13, "I do set my bow in the cloud, and it shall be for a token of a covenant between Me (God) and the earth."

Exodus 24:8, "And Moses took the blood and sprinkled it on the people and said, 'Behold the blood of the new covenant, which the Lord had made with you concerning all these words."

Matthew 26:28, "For this is My blood of the covenant, which is poured out for many for forgiveness of sins." (New American Standard version.)

It is the will of God that human beings should get into moral relationship with Him and His covenants are for this purpose. Why does God not save some? He has saved them, but they have not entered into a personal relationship with Him. They have not accepted the gift of their salvation. All the great blessings of God are finished and complete, but they are not mine until I enter into a personal relationship with Him based on His covenant.

"Waiting" for God to do something in me is incarnate unbelief and means I have no faith in Him. I wait for Him to do something in me and then I can trust in that. God will not do it because that is not the basis of the God/man relationship. Man must go out of himself in his covenant with God as God goes out of Himself with His covenant with man. It is a question of faith in God. We, instead, rely on our feelings. I do not believe God unless He will give me something in my hand where I may know I have it. Then I say, "Now I believe." Faith is not in operation. The Lord says: "Look unto Me and be saved." Isaiah 45:22

DIVINE INSPIRATION

I am writing this book because God inspired me to do so. My hope is that it blesses you! Many times I have asked Him what to say and how to say it--I need help as I have no special talent or merit of my own to do this. But God ….

I have been praying for more "divine inspiration," asking God to give me the perfect scriptures, key words and catch phrases that will inspire readers. My prayer is for His Holy Spirit to direct each reader personally. If you selected this book, you are most likely searching---looking for ways to start, improve or develop your prayer life.

When we are born again, we receive the Holy Spirit. Think of this as a small, hot coal that needs to be fanned. When born again, we go to the next level of our spiritual awakening --- the beginning of our Christian journey! Now the battle also begins. The enemy presses in to give us doubt ---- do we follow God or not? Do we go to church or not? Do we associate with our former friends who remain yet unsaved or align ourselves with fellow believers? The bible tells us not to be unevenly yoked, meaning saint and sinner. 2 Cor 6:14. This is especially important when you are newly born again and just beginning to learn God's ways and will. We do face choices and decisions and we are given free will. This is how our ancestors, going back to the garden with Adam and Eve, made the wrong choice!

Prayer is about improving your relationship with the Lord, which is your personal responsibility. No one else can do it for you. It's important to ask the Lord what is His will --- what does He want you to pray for. He will answer you in your spirit and through His word. As you advance, He will also sometimes use other believers to guide you. Everyone that crosses your path in life is there to teach you something.

I cannot emphasize enough how important it is to read your bible (and pray) on a regular, daily basis. Everything you need to know to grow is in that sacred book and is a direct connection to the Almighty God., who waits for you to begin the plans He has ordained for you alone. You can be certain He *always* hears your prayers. You may not like the answer, it may not be what you wanted, but God knows what is best for you and you must learn to trust Him completely.

Jeremiah 29:11-13, "For I know the plans that I have for you, declares the Lord, plans for welfare and not calamity to give you a future and a hope. Then you will call upon Me, and I will listen to you. And you will seek Me and find Me when you search for me with all your heart."

More things happen because of prayer than these the world dreams of. God cherishes the prayers of His children and longs to hear from every one of us! Prayer is the very foundation of your spiritual journey. If you could receive even a small glimpse of what your prayers could provide, you would be on your knees around the clock!

Every day, I remain in awe of the blessings God has given me and my family for our prayers. Looking back, it is hard for me to believe God has been so gracious to us with such multiple blessings. Our journey has been so beautiful since my wife and I gave our lives to Jesus. So different than it was before we were born again. We are ever thankful that God did indeed call us and we followed! Your life too, will change in most remarkable ways. It will make you wonder how you ever got through life without following Jesus, reading your bible and praying.

James 4:2, "We have not because we ask not."

Hosea 4:6, "My people die for lack of knowledge." (Knowledge of God's Word.)

James 5:13-16, "Is there any among you afflicted? Let him pray. Is any merry--let him sings psalms. Is any sick among you? Let him call for the elders of the church and let them pray over him, anointing him with oil in the Name of the Lord. And the prayer of faith shall save the sick and the Lord shall raise him up, and if he had committed any sins they shall be forgiven him. Confess your faults one to another and pray one for another, the effectual fervent prayer of a righteous man avails much."

Are you in right standing with God? If not, humble yourself before Him and pray. Your prayers will accomplish much.

THE NAME OF JESUS

John 14:13-14, "and whatsoever you shall ask in My name, that will I so that the Father may be glorified in the Son. If you ask me anything in My name, I will do it." This is a promise from God. The Christians power of attorney. It glorifies God to answer all prayers and save, heal and bless all men.

Some years back when my mother was in the hospital, it was necessary for me to have her power of attorney. I did not like it, but I had to pay bills and take care of her business. When Jesus ascended into heaven, He left His power of attorney with His disciples. John 14:12 gives these powers to all believers, but few use it. Until you have a personal revelation, you will not believe you have this power.

As a Pentecostal, the only way I pray is in the name of Jesus. I have been taught this from the start of my Christian walk. This is the appropriate way to pray to assure your prayers will be effective. The Bible tells us in Matt 10:33, "But whosoever shall deny Me (Jesus) before men, I also deny before My Father who is in heaven." I certainly do not want to be denied, do you?

I was once in a delicate situation at work. I had been warned about expressing my faith in the work place. A fellow employee was having a heart attack with the ambulance on it's way. I sat with this person quietly saying the Name of Jesus repeatedly. When he got to the ER, they could find nothing wrong with him! I gave God all the glory for using me as His instrument. We know there is power in the Name above all Names! The precious Name of Jesus of Nazareth --- the Name that saves, heals, delivers and causes demons to tremble. Use it often in your prayers with respect and authority.

There are many songs about the power of the name of Jesus. One mentions we should say the Name of Jesus when we do not know what to say (or pray.) The song continues to say there is *something* about that

Name. Those who do not have the gift of tongues can simply pray the Name of Jesus in any given situation. Many mothers softly pray the name of Jesus over their sleeping children for protection and blessings.

In Acts, chapter 3, Peter is at the gate called Beautiful, where he used the power of attorney for the first time. In verse 6 he says "In the Name of Jesus Christ of Nazareth, rise up and walk." And that man did indeed get up and walk after having been an invalid for many years. Then in Acts 4, Peter and John were arrested for proclaiming Jesus as healer of the man who was healed. So the priests, Sadducees and temple guard demanded to know "By what power or in what name have you done this?" (Acts 4:7) Whereas Peter, filled by the Holy Spirit replied, Acts 4:8-10, " Rulers and elders of the people, if we are on trial today for a benefit done to a sick man, as to how this man has been made well, let it be made known to all of you, and to all the people of Israel, that by the name of

Jesus Christ the Nazarene, whom you crucified, whom God raised from the dead--by this name this man stands here before you in good health."

In Acts 4:18 they commanded Peter and John not to speak at all or teach in the Name of Jesus. As it says in Ecclesiastes 1:9, "there is nothing new under the sun," as today the Name of Jesus is still being banned. The enemy has not given up trying to stop God's work since Genesis!

Yes, there is something extremely special and sacred about the mighty Name of our Lord and Savior, Jesus Christ of Nazareth.

Believers have authority in the name of Jesus—let's use it! Amen!

THE PRAYER LIFE OF JESUS

Jesus is our role model and we should strive to be as much like Him as we can. We are called Christians, which means Little Christs. In His human form, Jesus was the best teacher there ever was and continues to be our source and divine inspiration. He has risen---He is alive and is forever with us! Hallelujah!

Mark 1:35, "And in the morning, rising up a great while before the day, Jesus went out and departed into a solitary place, and there prayed." This was His habit--- to arise before daylight, to be alone with God.

Psalm 5:3 (Psalm of David), David prayed "My voice shall Thou hear in the morning, O Lord in the morning will I direct my prayer unto Thee and will look up." David, like Jesus, rose early to be with God. Reported he is a man who had a heart for God.

This is a great way to start your day. Before anything else, go to the Father and you will be blessed.

Matt 14:23, "And when He had sent the multitudes away, Jesus went up into the mountain alone to pray; and when it was evening, He was there alone." As it says in Mark 4:10; 6:47; Luke 9:18; 36 and John 6:15:

Jesus spent long hours alone with God. His private praying and conquest of Satan were the secrets of His public power. It was through prayer that He received the Holy Spirit:

Luke 3:22, ..."and the Holy Spirit descended upon Him in bodily form like a dove, and a voice came out of heaven: Thou art My beloved Son, in Thee I am well pleased." By continued prayer, Jesus received fresh anointing of the Spirit for His daily work. He used the same methods to get and keep power that are required of believers. We are cracked pots --- we leak and need to be refilled! Give us this day our daily infilling of the Holy Spirit is not a onetime deal. As we pour out, we need to be constantly refilled and refreshed.

Matt 26:36, "Then Jesus came with them to a place called Gethsemane and said to His disciples, *sit here while I go over there and pray.*" It is said here that Jesus was in such deep, fervent prayer that His sweat became drops of blood falling to the ground from His forehead. There are many pictures showing this scene. There was a spiritual battle going on and Jesus needed the strength to make it to the cross. He was to drink the cup. He prayed: (Luke 22:42) "Father, if Thou art willing, remove this cup from Me; yet not My will but Thine be done."

Matt 6:6 tells us not to be on display or show off (show others how "spiritual" we are) when we pray. Verse 7 reminds us of vain repetitions. There is a difference between persistence and repetitions. For example, saying the Lord's Prayer many times with no feeling or saying it once from your heart. Once a single prayer request is presented to God, we can then thank Him for His answer repeatedly. Mark 11:23-25 instructs to Pray, believe and receive. Keep in mind, you will not always receive the answer you expected, but God always knows best and we must always trust Him. There is a difference between firm, authoritative prayer and rude, demanding prayer. Go to the Almighty with a very humble heart, remembering how much God loves us.

Luke 11:9-10, "And I say unto you, ASK and it shall be given to you, SEEK and you shall find, KNOCK and it will be opened to you. For everyone that asks receives and he that seeks finds, and he that knocks, it shall be opened." How long should you pray for the same thing? Only God knows the answer to that. No one else can tell you. Sometimes it would be years before you receive an answer. Sometimes, the answer is just "no."

We must discipline ourselves to try to meet with God at the same time daily. There are, of course, always exceptions, but if you miss your appointment, be sure to at least pray when the time permits---do not just skip your prayer and bible reading that day. It is good to keep a journal. Record what you hear God's Holy Spirit saying to you, and record your own thoughts. It is encouraging to go back, read your journal, and see how God is working in your life. Try not to rush---time spent reading the Word and praying is more precious than anything else you will do in a day. Talk to the Lord--- tell Him everything on your heart and do not be concerned about any particular way of talking. God wants relationship with you---not any kind of regulation. Be honest, humble and sincere.

The same spirit that raised Jesus from the dead is in us. Romans 8:9-11.

My prayer for you is to be excited about your prayer time. Enjoy the great privilege we have as Christians to fellowship with God daily. In Jesus's name, we pray. Amen.

GREATER WORKS

Are You Ready to do Them?

John 14:12, "***Verily, verily I say unto you, he that believeth on me, the works that I do shall he do also and Greater Works than these shall he do because I go to the Father.***"

Taken from My Utmost for His Highest, by Oswald Chambers, Oct. 17 reading:

"*Prayer does not fit us for the greater works; prayer is the Greater work. We think of prayer as a common-sense exercise of our higher powers in order to prepare us for God's work. In the teaching of Jesus Christ prayer is the working of the miracle of redemption in me, which produces the miracle of redemption in others by the power of God. The way fruit remains is by prayer, but remember it is prayer based on the agony of redemption, not on my agony. Only a child gets prayer answered; a wise man does not.*

Prayer is the battle. It is a matter of indifference where you are. Whichever way God engineer's circumstances, the duty is to pray. Do not allow the thought: "I am of no use where I am" because you certainly can be of no use where you are not. Wherever God has dumped you down in circumstances pray to Him all the time. "Whatsoever ye ask in My name, that will I do." John 14:13. We won't pray unless we get thrills, that is the most intense form of spiritual selfishness. We have to labor along the line of God's direction, and He says pray. "Pray ye therefore the Lord of the harvest, that He will send forth laborers into His harvest." Luke 10:2.

There is nothing thrilling about a laboring man's work, but it is the laboring man who makes the conceptions of genius possible and it is the laboring saint who makes the conceptions of his Master possible. You labor at prayer and results happen all the time from His standpoint. What an astonishment it will be to find, when the veil is lifted, the souls that have been reaped by you, simply because you had been in the habit of taking your orders from Jesus Christ."

The Greater Works are not those of reaching more people by means of television, radio, the internet and the printed page, for these are natural means and can be used by unsaved men who do not have the Holy Spirit power to do the works of Christ. No man can receive greater power than Christ can, therefore, the Greater Works could not consist of doing greater things than Christ could have done had He had the occasion to do them. The thought is that each believer can have equal power with Christ to do what He did as well as greater things if and when the occasion would require.

Romans 8:11, " But if the Spirit of Him that raised up Jesus from the dead dwell in you He that raised up Christ from the dead shall also quicken your mortal bodies by His Spirit that dwells in you."

To reiterate, the same Spirit that raised our Lord, Jesus Christ from the dead, dwells in us! Hallelujah! Praise the Lord! We have the power and authority from Christ --- let's use it!

I pray for God's Holy Spirit to open your eyes so you see the plans He has for you and that you use the precious gifts He has given you.

In Jesus Name, I pray, amen.

GOSPEL OF JOHN

John, The Beloved Disciple

We are all familiar with the artist's rendition of the "Last Supper" where, in the painting, there is a disciple with his head resting on Jesus's shoulder. Do you know who this disciple is? Yes, John was about 18 or 19 years old at the time of the last supper. He started following Jesus at 15 or 16 so he was very young among the other disciples. In fact, some of the other disciples could have been his father.

John was special, thus his gospel is also special as well as sacred. He was in his 80's when he wrote Revelation. Theologians and bible scholars affirm we don't know the chronological order of John's writings so we follow the order they are presented in the bible.

When Jesus was on the cross, John was the only original disciple present. John 19:26-27, "He (Jesus) looked down at His mother and said, 'Woman behold thy son.' He then said to John, 'behold thy mother.'" From that moment on, John took full responsibility for Mary, taking her into his home. (Joseph had already died.) At the young age of about 19 John was given the awesome responsibility (and blessing) of caring for God's mother!

What an awesome privilege! John was certainly special to Jesus.

Of the four Gospels, John is the easiest to understand and to read. Matthew wrote for the Jews, as did Mark who also wrote for the Romans, and Luke wrote for the Greeks. John wrote for everyone.

Literary scholars past and present do not all believe in God. Some are atheists, some agnostics some skeptics, but they all agree the Gospel of John is excellent. Everything that is written in the Gospel of John--the history, sermons and prophesies, as well as its presentation, is considered the Gospel of the Divine One --- Lord Jesus Christ.

You may be confused as to which translation of the bible is best for you to read. You can pray and ask God to give you confirmation on which one is best suited to your level of understanding and ease in reading. You may want to start with a student edition, which is one that gives much commentary to help you understand what scripture really means. Again, pray for divine intervention to lead you to the right choice for you. The important thing is to read the Word daily.

Some bibles will give you a plan to read it in one year. That, of course, does not mean to not continue to read it! Personally, I have been on the one-year plan for over 10 years and it never ceases to amaze me that even though I have read the scriptures many times, I get something new frequently. The Word of God is alive and it will speak to you, personally. The same scripture can meet you at different places in your spiritual growth, giving you fresh knowledge and insight. Perhaps a "word in season."

The bible is God's Word written by mans' hand. Holy Scripture, divinely inspired.

God said it, I believe it, that settles it!

Nothing else even comes to the divine message of the bible. Keep it alongside of your bed--fall asleep reading it and letting God's Word seep into your spirit. You will be blessed, as God's Word does not come back void. (Isaiah 55:11.)

I pray that you will stay in the Word daily.

In Jesus's name, I pray. Amen.

THE HOUSE OF PRAYER

Matt 21:13, "It is written, MY HOUSE SHALL BE CALLED A HOUSE OF PRAYER."

This is Jesus speaking. He said this after He cleaned out the Temple of the moneychangers and merchants.

It is no coincidence that as I was working on this book on prayer when our church was attempting to set a precedent to increase prayer in the church. Back on January 1, 2009 a week of special prayer and special daily and weekly prayer meetings were kicked off. The need had been recognized, as there was so much to pray for when looking ahead at the uncertainty of the New Year. This is still true today! Our senior Pastor had encouraged everyone to pray according to the bible --- pray without ceasing. (1 Thes 5:17) Everyone should consider doing this in his or her church, starting with leadership, to emphasize the importance of prayer.

Prayer binds Satan ---ties him up. It releases God's angels sending them to work. Prayer people will tell you, prayer is the first, second and third thing that needs to be done on a daily basis. There are few churches and Christians that are devoted to prayer. Many will get on their knees when they have a need or crisis, but fail to pray when all is well. Prayer, however, is so important and we all need to be praying as if our lives and those we pray for are dependent on it because they are!

James 5:16, "*The effectual fervent prayer of a righteous man availed much.*" You may ask, "OK, so who are righteous men?" He who is in right standing with God. Your next question could possibly be then how do you accomplish this. You need to believe in the Lord, Jesus Christ --- that He died for you, was raised from the dead, and is the living God. That Jesus died so we may live, taking all sins of humankind upon Himself. Having accepted this truth, you can then ask the Father if there is anything He wants you, personally to do and listen for that still quiet voice. God will never let you down.

Let's look at the word, "fervent." Webster's dictionary says "fiery, intense, passionate, eager, with feeling. WOW! Are your prayers like that? They can be.

Prayer --- a divinely devised means of releasing God's heavenly power in your life. It is the simplest yet most profound form of communication with the Father. God promises, in Jeremiah 33:3, "Call unto Me and I will answer thee, and show thee great and mighty things which thou knowest not." 2 Chron 7:14, "If My people, which are called by My name, shall humble themselves and pray, and seek My face, and turn from their sin, I will heal their land." This is surely a word in season when you look at the condition of the world today.

Prayer changes things. It moves the hand of God. We have established that our prayers are needed and will get a whole lot done!

TWENTY-THREE ELEMENTS OF THE LORD'S PRAYER

The Model Prayer

Matthew 6:9-13, "We are commanded to pray in this manner, using this as a model for all prayers."

23 elements of the Lord's Prayer:

1. Relationship: Our Father

2. Recognition: who art in heaven

3. Adoration: hallowed be thy name

4. Anticipation: Thy kingdom come

5. Consecration: Thy will be done

6. Universality: on earth

7. Conformity: as it is in heaven

8. Supplication: give us

9. Definiteness: this day

10. Necessity: our daily bread

11. Penitence: and forgive us

12. Obligation: our debts

13. Forgiveness: as we forgive

14. Love and Mercy: our debtors

15. Guidance: and lead us

16. Protection: not into temptation

17. Salvation: but deliver us

18. Righteousness: from evil

19. Faith: for Thine is the kingdom

20. Humility: and the power

21. Reverence: and the glory

22. Timelessness: for ever

23. Affirmation: amen

The first three petitions of the prayer make 7 points concerning God; the last four petitions make 16 points concerning man.

The end of verse 13, "For Thine is the kingdom and the power and the glory forever…," is omitted by various denominations, Catholic being one of them.

When we *pray, praise, repent, ask, yield,* we are praying the Lord's perfect prayer. We are commanded to pray this way. Using this prayer as our model helps us to know that we are in line with Jesus' teaching. When the disciples asked Him how to pray, this was His instruction, to pray the Lord 's Prayer.

Start and end your day with the Lord's Prayer, with meaning from your heart. As Christians, one of our greatest privileges is to call God "Our Father." Another is to pray to Him.

Pray aloud as when we recite scriptures we chase away any unsavory elements that may want to bother us. As always, we pray in the precious, holy name of Jesus, the name above all names; the name that heals, delivers, saves and sends the enemy running. Amen!

DAILY PRAYER

Taken from the hymn, "What a Friend We Have in Jesus" by Joseph Scriver, circa 1855:

"Oh what peace we often forfeit, what needless pain we bear all because we do not carry everything to God in prayer."

Proverbs 16:3, "Commit thy works unto the Lord, and thy thoughts shall be established."

This is a promise and a command from God. In other words, if we take God into partnership with us, our plans will succeed!

How do you start your day? When I say my daily morning prayers, I list all that is planned for the day. I routinely say Proverbs 16:3, as I cannot think of a better way to begin. Granted, not all is always "smooth sailing." If I run into a speed bump, a closed door, I will stop and pray, thanking God for the delay, as there is most likely a good reason for it. God wants us to involve Him in the small stuff as well as the big stuff. Most of the time, the small things are building blocks for bigger things.

With understanding, it is comforting to realize God is with us with our every move. His Holy Spirit is one with our spirit. We have an anointing in measure with our tasks for the day.

How to begin? Those of you reading this that are not praying on a regular basis may be confused. We are required (obligated for our own benefit) to pray daily, as well as read the bible. The bible instructs us, in Psalm 5:3, to pray in the morning: "My voice shalt thou hear in the morning, O Lord, in the morning will I direct my prayer unto Thee and will look up."

If your only prayers are over your food or in church, you need to develop new habits. Start small: "Good morning God, it is Me. Thank you for being with me today, blessing me and my family and those that I should pray for. Thank you for your Holy Spirit who guides me, helping me with every choice and decision. In Jesus' name I pray." Then during the day, if you have some down time--- being on line, stuck in traffic etc. pray! Pray the Lord's Prayer and pray for what is on your heart. The Lord's Prayer covers everything. "Give us this day our daily bread" means to give us what we need for that day---not just bread but things like housing, clothing, help with finances--- whatever it is you are in need of. "Deliver us from evil" In the Greek, evil comes from penos which means sin, sickness and poverty, all things we want protection and deliverance from!

How long should you pray? That is an individual thing. Of course, it can depend on how much time you can afford. Working people and young mothers have little free time. But what you are willing to set aside for time with God is the most important time spent.

Smith Wigglesworth was a great man of prayer. A common man, he was a spiritual giant. When questioned how long he prayed, he answered 5 minutes. How could this great man of God pray only 5 minutes? He continued to explain that he prayed for 5 minutes, went about his work for 5 minutes, then prayed again for 5 minutes. This practice continued all through his day.

Kenneth Hagin, Sr., founder of REMA Bible College, was often observed praying in tongues while watching TV!

Different levels --different devils. The enemy does not want you to pray. He will continuously divert your attention to discourage you from prayer. This is good reason why you should make an effort to get up early enough --- before there is any activity going on in your household, and pray. Spend that quality time with God. It is not a question of IF you will be attacked by the enemy of your soul, it is *when*. You need your spiritual covering always in place.

Psalm 91:1, "I (insert your name) will dwell in the secret place of the most High and abide under the shadow of the Almighty." This is where you want to spend your day----spend your life--- under God's protection. What an awesome God we serve, amen? Copy this psalm down and recite it every day---aloud if you can.

Psalm 91:11, "For You, (God) shall give your angels charge over me, (your name), to keep me in all my ways." God loves us so much He gives us guardian angels to protect us. We must always give Him thanks and praise.

P. U. S. H.

PRAY UNTIL SOMETHING HAPPENS

There is power in persevering prayer. We all know the parable of the unjust judge in Luke:18:1-8 (NAS version—Jesus is talking to His disciples), "Now He was telling them a parable to show that at all times they ought to pray and not lose heart saying *"there was in a certain city a judge that did not fear God, and did not respect man. And there was a widow in that city and she kept coming to him, saying, 'Give me legal protection from my opponent.' And for a while he was unwilling; but afterward he said to himself,' Even though I do not fear God or respect man, yet because this widow bothers me, I will give her legal protection , lest by continually coming she wear me out.' And the Lord said Hear what the unrighteous judge said ' now shall not God bring about justice for His elect, who cry to Him day and night, and will He delay long over them? I tell you that He will bring about justice for them speedily. However, when the Son of Man comes, will He find faith on earth?"*

Do not give in to fear, doubt, unbelief and discouragement or use excuses for unbelief when prayer is not answered immediately. We are to rebuke and resist all opposition and suggestion of failure. It is a divine blood-bought right to get an answer, so do not lose heart. The above-mentioned widow was very irritating to the judge. He only helped her because she was wearing him out. The squeaky wheel gets the oil! Luke 18:7-8 is a promise from God and ALL God's promises are yes and amen (2 Cor 1:20) ---- His word does not come back void. (Isaiah 55:11).

How long do we have to P.U.S.H.? Only God knows the answer to that question. You need to ask Him in prayer. His answer will come in a way you may not expect.

I know a true story of a Pastor with an older, unsaved brother. This Pastor prayed for his brother for 26 years. Finally, the brother was on his deathbed at 84--full of cancer and in terrible pain. The Pastor told him he prays the Lord would not let him die until he accepted Jesus as Lord and Savior. Romans 10:9, "Confess with your mouth that Jesus is Lord, and believe in your heart that God raised Him from the dead and you shall be saved." The next day he finally did accept Jesus as Lord and savior and a day later, he went home to the Lord. Because of this Pastor's diligent, continuous prayer, God had mercy on his brother.

VAIN REPETITIONS

Matt 6:7 NIV (This is Jesus speaking), "*And when you pray, do not keep on babbling like pagans, for they think they will be heard because of their many words.*"

This is a command from God telling us not to use vain repetitions. God hears us the first time we pray. Repeating the same prayer repeatedly would be for our purpose so that we can "set it" in our own minds. What I do after the initial prayer is said, I continually thank God for granting me the request.

Mark 11:23-24, "*I tell you the truth, if anyone says to this mountain, 'Go, throw yourself into the sea,' and does not doubt in his heart but believes that what he says will happen, it will be done for him. Therefore, I tell you, whatever you ask for in prayer, believe that you have received it and it will be yours.*" This states pray, believe and receive. Even though you do not (yet) have what you are praying for, keep thanking God as if you already received it. This is where faith is demonstrated. Jesus said many times, "Oh you of little faith" (Matt 8:26) which refers to any Christian doubter.

If you repeat the Lord's Prayer each day-- sometimes more than once, and it is sincere and coming from the love in your heart for the Father, you have prayed more in that day, than many other Christians! This is not vain repetition--- this is honoring your Holy Father, as it is the prayer Jesus himself taught us to pray. The word "vain" means empty or useless, so Jesus is warning us that repeating worthless phrases in our prayers will not help them be heard by God. Our Heavenly Father is not concerned with word count, flowery expressions or mantras; He desires "truth in the inward being." (Psalm 51:6 ESV). No one knows our heart except God. Learn to be humbly honest with Him always.

When praying for a specific person, situation or circumstance, you can thank God as much as you feel you need to. He never tires of our thanks. When someone gives you a gift, don't you thank them? How much more then should we be thankful to God who is moving mountains for us, giving us the desires of our hearts? Please understand, you must be within God's will and walking in His service, not expecting to be showered with unreasonable and outlandish requests! Ps 100:4-5 *"Enter His gates with thanksgiving and His courts with praise; give thanks to Him and praise His name. For the Lord is good and His love endures forever; His faithfulness continues through all generations."*

Matt 6:8 says our Father knows what we need before we ask Him. So why should we ask?

Good question. The Lord tells us we have not because we ask not or seek not. (Matt 7:7)

I was born and raised Catholic, so I attended a Catholic grade school. Every year it was a ritual for me to ask my Dad for book money for school. He knew he had to give it to me, but he wanted me to ask him for it, and so I did. I had to wait for him to be in a good mood. Every year, it was the same scenario--he would give me the speech on how tight money was and I had to listen to the entire speech, and then thank him for the money. A major contrast is our Heavenly Father is available *always* and is *always* loving and gracious, but we still need to ask and thank Him. We have absolutely no reason not to!

As a note here, I eventually left the Catholic faith, and continued my spiritual journey as a born again Christian, now membered in a Pentecostal church. God does indeed direct our path!

We are all aware of how much money we have in our checking accounts. Say you have $100.00 in the bank. You know you can write a check for $95.00 without a problem, so you write the check and collect $95.00 cash from the teller. How much would you say you have in your spiritual account? Enough to cover that last prayer request? As you become more involved in prayer, your faith will grow and you will have the confidence to understand that certain prayers will indeed be honored, i.e. a "gimme." Any golfers reading this knows a gimme is when a ball is so close to the hole, you get credit for it without hitting the ball. It's a shot that the other players agree can count automatically without being played.

A friend of mine was healed of deafness in his right ear. As a result of this, many others having hearing problems that he prayed for were also healed. His faith allowed God to bless him with this special gift. I have had similar experiences. Certain prayer requests are a gimme. At Teen Challenge, where I teach once a week, one popular prayer request is favor with the courts and the judge. Many are in the TC program instead of jail. Over a four-year period, we have had a 95% success rate on prayers for all in these situations. This is a faith builder for all we pray for!

Years back on a church prayer team, my wife and I stood in agreement with a distressed grandmother whose grandson was looking at a 10-year jail term. Weeks later, she gave the praise report he was released with a lesser sentence. Praise God! Another grandmother in the church started to cry as her grandson had receive a 10-year term of hard time. The two young men had such a similar history, it was unbelievable. The difference was we had prayed for one and not the other. The grandmother who was crying was too embarrassed to ask. We have not for we ask not.

I always tell my students, the only stupid question is the one not asked. Similarly, there are no stupid prayer requests. Listen to your heart and pray for everything you can.

At times, we are given discernment. We understand that there are circumstances when a simple, single line prayer is sufficient and all that is necessary. Other times, we may not be sure of how long to pray or what to say even. This is when tongues is so helpful. You can use your gift of a heavenly language to allow the Holy Spirit to completely take over and say the prayers you are unequipped to utter yourself.

The Jabez Prayer books by Bruce Wilkinson gives us powerful insight into what and how to pray. My wife and I have used the 30 day pray plan with great success. It is a life changer:

Prayer of Jabez:

"Oh that you would bless me indeed, and enlarge my territory, that your hand would be with me and that you would keep me from evil that I may NOT cause pain."

Large asking and large expectation on our part honors God. (Edmund Nelson).

I was at a ministers' meeting several years ago where there were 40-50 Men of God in one room together and witnessed His glory. We were going around the room sharing testimonies. A large missionary, just back from the field shared with us that arriving home, he needed a car. When he prayed, he recognized God telling him to pray for 30 days. On the 30th day, there was a knock on his door and a man handed him a set of car keys to the car parked in front of his house! It was not new, but it surely would serve the purpose. He praised and worshiped God! Some weeks later, the home he was renting sold and he had to move. He again prayed for 30 days, as instructed, once again, by God. Another knock on his door brought another man with the keys to a house. The house was small, but adequate. WOW!! We were now all praising God, and acknowledging nothing is impossible with our Father! After lunch, this missionary was gone. When talking to the pastors who had been sitting along side of him, none of them knew him or had seen him before. It was not uncommon for us to have guests. Was he an angel, sent by God to boost our faith? We will never know…..

Begin to use the 30 day prayer of Jabez. If a longer period is required, then P.U.S.H.—prayer until something happens.

Prayer is a battle as shown in Daniel, chapter 10. It is the only time in the bible a battle is described between angels and the devil (Prince of

Persia). Michael had begun this battle with evil then he needed Gabriel to come to his aide for the victory. I picture this battle with many legions on both sides. We know not what our prayers accomplish, but we do know God loves us so much He gives us angels to have charge over us. Ps 91:11. I thank God daily for the angels He sends to protect me as I am about the Father's business.

Keep praying without losing heart --- especially for salvation of family members! Our timing is not God's timing. Be patient knowing God is always faithful--He will answer your every prayer.

DIFFERENT TYPES OF PRAYER

1. PRAISE: God for what He has done is doing and will do. Psalm 66

2. WORSHIP: God for who He is, His character. 1 Chronicles 16:23-31

3. THANKSGIVING: All His acts; acknowledgement. 1 Thessalonians 5:18; Psalm 100:4 (These are only two examples. Thanksgiving comes up many times in the bible.)

4. COMMITMENT: Give all to Him, relinquishment. Proverbs 16:3

5. PETITION: Ask, Seek, Knock … Matt 7:7

6. PERSEVERANCE: *P.U.S.H* Pray until something happens. Luke 18:7-8 and 1Thes. 5:17

7. INTERCESSION: Pray for others. Job 42:10

8. AGREEMENT: Two or more standing in agreement. Matt 18:19-20

9. GOD'S WORD: Using scripture specifically. ALL scripture as written in the bible. For example, when praying for healing, recite His promises pertaining to healing such as in Isaiah 53:5 "*…and by His stripes, we are healed.*"

10. PRAYING IN THE SPIRIT: Praying in tongues. 1Cor 14:2

To put it simply, most times, we will pray either for others or for ourselves.

As you develop your own personal relationship with God, He will help you.

You need to pray daily, frequently, and from your heart.

Be serious about your prayers and God will be serious about answering them. Remember too, the answer won't always be what you expected or wanted, but God always answers in what is best for you.

Trust Him always and completely. He loves you and wants fellowship with you. Prayer is simply talking to Him. Isn't that awesome? Just talking to Almighty God! There are even times when you need not say anything---just listen. Listen for His still, quiet voice in your spirit and be blessed.

Some of these teachings will tend to be repetitious because they need to be.

May God bless you abundantly!

10 CONDITIONS TO ANSWERED PRAYER

Taken from page 47 of the Dake Bible (New Testament) Mark 11:23

This is a *prophesy* and a *promise* from God.

1. ***HAVE THE FAITH OF GOD:***

   Romans 4:17; Hebrews 11:3; Galatians 5:22-23

2. ***PRAY-- SAY IN NO UNCERTAIN TERMS WHAT YOU WANT:***

   Mark 11:23-24; Matt 17:20 and 21:21-22; John 15:7

3. ***HAVE UNLIMITED FAITH WITHOUT QUALIFYING OR LIMITING GOD'S WILL OR WHAT YOU WANT:***

   Mark 11:23-24; Matt 17:20 and 21:21-22; John 15:7 (#2 and 3 are the same verses)

4. ***REFUSE TO DOUBT IN THE HEART:***

   Mark 11:23; Matt 17:20; John 1:5-8 (some verses are duplicated)

5. ***BELIEVE THAT WHATEVER IS ASKED WILL BE GIVEN:***

   Mark 11:23-24; Matt 7:7-11 and 17:20 and 21:21-22; Hebrews 11:6

6. ***BELIEVE THAT WHATEVER IS ASKED IS ALREADY GRANTED:***

   Mark 11:24; Matt 17:20; 1 John 5:14-15

7. ***BE AUTHORITATIVE AND COMMAND TO COME TO PASS WHAT IS ASKED:***

Mark 11:23-24 and 9:23; Matt 17:20

8. ***BELIEVE THAT WHAT YOU WANT IS GOD'S WILL:***

Mark 11:23-24; John 15:7; Matt 17:20 and 21:21-22; Hebrews 11:6; James 1:5-8

9. ***NEVER SAY "IF IT BE THY WILL" CONCERNING ANYTHING YOU ASK THAT IS DEFINITELY PROMISED OF GOD IN HIS WORD:***

Mark 11:23; Psalms 84:11; 2 Cor 1:20; and 2 Peter 1:3-4

10. ***HAVE A CLEAN HEART AND LIFE WITH GOD AND MAN:***

Mark 11:25; John 15:7; 1 John 3:22-23

"Whatsoever," "Anything," "All things," "What ye will," "What things soever ye desire," "Whatsoever He saith," and other unlimited terms are found, assuring the absolute certainty of, and the possibilities of answered prayer.

DRINK! STEAL! SWEAR! LIE!

DRINK: From the everlasting cup daily.

STEAL: A moment to help others worse off then you are.

SWEAR: To be a better person today then I was yesterday.

LIE: Down at night thanking God for all your blessings.

I am not as good as I should be.

I am not as good as I can be.

But thanks to God, I pray that I am better than I was.

Success is sweet—it's secret is sweat!

Author unknown.

To be a better person today. When you haven't been your best, always have the attitude: Today I failed but tomorrow I will try again. Tomorrow I will succeed.

When you are thanking God for your blessings--- be sure to include not only those that you are presently enjoying, but all the blessings you are yet to receive!

TEN (SCRIPTURAL) RESPONSIBILITIES OF CHRISTIANS

Key Scripture: Acts 5:42 --- Amplified Bible version:

*"**Yet** (in spite of the threats) **they** (Apostles) **never ceased for a single day, both in the temple area and at home, to teach and to proclaim the good news** (Gospel) **of Jesus** (the Messiah.)"*

1. Pray daily: (Prayer for what we need daily. "Give us this day, our daily bread.")   Matt 6:11 and Luke 11:3

2. Take up our daily cross: "And He (Jesus) was saying to them all, *"If anyone wishes to come after Me, let him deny himself, and take up his cross **daily**, and follow Me."* Luke 9:23.

3. Continue in one accord: "And day by day continuing with one mind in the temple, and breaking bread from house to house, they were taking their meals together with gladness and sincerity of heart." Acts 2:46

4. Teach: As Christians, it is important for us to reflect on key messages in the Bible to reiterate our purpose of sharing the Word of God on earth. Several verses in Scripture tell us clearly that God expects us to spread His Word to everyone in the world. From the joyous hymns of Psalms to the accounts of the disciples in Matthew and Mark, there can be no doubt that we as Christians have an essential duty to fulfill on earth. Mark 16:15 NKJV, "And He said to them, *"Go into all the world and preach the gospel to every creature."*

5. Win Souls: Proverbs 11:30, "The fruit of the righteous is a tree of life, and he who is wise wins souls." And Daniel 12:3, "Those who have insight will shine like the brightness of heaven, and those who lead the many to righteousness, like the stars forever and ever."

6. Preach Jesus: Acts 5:42, " And every day, in the temple and from house to house, they (apostles) kept right on teaching and preaching Jesus as the Christ." We are to follow that example and tell others about Jesus.

7. Search the Scriptures: John 5:39 (NAS), "You search the scriptures because you think that in them you have eternal life; it is these that testify about Me."

8. Discuss Scriptures: Ezekiel 33:30, "but as for you, son of man, your fellow citizens who talk about you by the walls and in the doorways of the houses, speak to one another, each to his brother saying 'Come now and hear what the message is which comes from the Lord.' and Luke 24:14-15, "And they were talking with each other about all these things which had taken place. While they were talking and discussing, Jesus Himself approached and began traveling with them."

9. Carry Responsibility: Galations 6:4-5, "But let each one test his own work, and then his reason to boast will be in himself alone and not in his neighbor. For each will have to bear his own load." And Romans 14:10 & 12 " for we will all stand before the judgment seat of God. So then each of us will give an account of himself to God."

10. Exhort One Another: Hebrews 3:13, " But encourage one another day after day, as long as it is still called today, lest any of you be hardened by the deceitfulness of sin."

This was a continued ministry of the Apostles in spite of opposition.

It is my hope that you understand that daily prayer and bible reading are not optional, but "required" for your own good and especially for your spiritual growth. Living this way will bless you abundantly as you draw nearer to God.

"....Do not be just hearers of the Word, but doers..." James 1:22

THINGS I <u>ALWAYS</u> NEED TO DO:

1. Praise God!

2. Pray without ceasing

3. Pray for others

4. Pray for myself

5. Stay in His Word every day

6. Plead the Blood of Christ--apply the blood to myself and loved ones

7. Walk in the fear of the Lord

8. Build my faith constantly

9. Be always, ALWAYS thankful--develop an attitude of gratitude

10. STOP COMPLAINING! Complaining says I do not trust God and opens a door for the enemy.

11. Do not "conform" to this world. We (Christians) are IN this world, not OF it.

12. Keep a positive attitude

13. Stop criticizing, judging, gossiping--everything negative and ugly.

14. Ask God what He wants of me daily

15. Honor the authority placed above me (my pastor, my president, my boss etc.)

16. Stop cursing! Words COUNT! Ask God to cleanse my mouth!

17. Gain--pray for--believe for self-control

18. Be kind--not rude. Love others.

19. Concentrate on Jesus and not any negative circumstances

20. Cast my burdens upon the Lord

21. Do NOT open any doors for the enemy through willful sin

22. Always, always, always be aware of my thoughts, words and actions and be a good witness.

KNOW GOD:

1. LOVES ME! Romans 8:37-39

2. Will never leave or forsake me Hebrews 13:5

3. Sends His angels to surround and protect me Ps 91:11

4. Defines WHO I am in Christ 1 Peter 2:9

5. Assures me "I can do all things through Christ who strengthens me" Phil 4:13

6. It's not by MY strength, but by HIS ....Zechariah 4:6

"....Do not be just hearers of the Word, but doers..." James 1:22

SEVEN STEPS TO ANSWERED PRAYER

1. Pray to the Father: John 16:23, "And in that day you shall ask Me nothing. Verily, verily I say unto you, 'Whatsoever you shall ask the father in My name, He will give it to you."

2. In the Name of Jesus: John 14:14, "If you shall ask anything in My Name, I will do it."

3. By the Holy Spirit: Romans 8:26, "Likewise the Spirit also helps our infirmities; for we know not what we should pray for as we ought, but the Spirit Itself makes intercession for us with groaning that can not be uttered."

4. With the full understanding of rights and privileges: 1 Cor 14:14-15, "For if I pray in an unknown tongue, my spirit prays, but my mind is unfruitful. What is the outcome then? I shall pray with the Spirit and I shall pray with the mind also; I shall sing with the Spirit and I shall sing with the mind also."

5. In harmony with the Word: ***If you abide in Me and My Words abide in you,*** you shall ask what you will and it shall be done unto you." (Pray according to God's will.)

It must be understood you cannot be deliberately living in any kind of sin and expect God to answer all your prayers. You must be walking with Him and ABIDING in Him.

6. In faith nothing doubting: James 1:6, "But let him ask in faith, nothing wavering, for he that wavers is like a wave on the sea driven with the wind and tossed."

7. With praise for the answer: Phil 4:6, "Be anxious for nothing but by everything with prayer and supplication with thanksgiving let your requests be made known to God."

EXAMPLE:

Father God, in Jesus Name I pray for _____. I know it says in your Word in 2 Peter 3:9 You wish none to perish. I stand on your Word in James 1:6 believing in faith (not wavering) that it is already done! In Jesus Name with thanksgiving, amen.

If you have the gift of tongues, you can add a prayer with the help of Holy Spirit. After we have prayed in the natural, we can enlist Holy Spirit, through tongues, to pray through us the way God would have us pray, as He alone knows what is needed for our prayers to be complete and effective.

James 5:15-16, " And the prayer of faith shall save the sick, and the Lord shall raise him up and if he had committed any sins they shall be forgiven him. Confess your faults to one another, pray for one another that you may be healed. The effectual, fervent prayer of a righteous man avails much."

Righteous means a 90 degree right angle, to be squared away with God; right standing in His eyes. These prayers will get a whole lot done. If you are not getting results, ask the Father why--what is holding you back. He will help you understand. Listen for His council through Holy Spirit. You will gain spiritual insight. Sometimes the barrier may be something you never thought of, or realized was out of balance or wrong. All the more reason to read the Word daily and seek the Lord's wisdom.

In Jesus name, I pray for you to be in right standing with God.

Amen.

ONE OF THE BEST DEFINITIONS OF PRAYER IN SCRIPTURE
1 Samuel 1:15-16

"And Hannah answered and said: *"No my Lord, I am a woman oppressed in spirit; I have drunk neither wine no strong spirit, but I have poured out my soul before the Lord. Do not consider your maidservant as a worthless woman; for I have spoken until now out of my great concern and provocation."* NAS version.

This is a good example of how to pray. Prayer should come from the abundance of the heart from which comes the issues of life.

Luke 6:45, *"A good man out of the good treasure of his heart brings forth what is good; and evil man out of the evil treasure of his heart brings forth what is evil, for; his mouth speaks that which fills his heart."* (This was Jesus speaking.)

The Marines are always looking for a few good men. The movie made from that title has a compelling line stating: "You can't handle hearing the truth." All men labeled "good" are not necessarily "good!"

Part of my testimony, circa May 1966: I went to a small chapel to pray as I was about to begin my basic training in the Army, destination: Vietnam. God and I had been strangers for some time. It was late at night and a small lamp illuminated a wooden cross on the wall behind the altar. It was very quiet as the chapel was empty except for me. I felt the presence of God. I just sat at first, then got on my knees. I cannot remember my exact words as that was so long ago, but I know I prayed from my heart, baring my soul to God. I put out a fleece.

The concept of "putting out a fleece" comes from the story of Gideon, a leader in Israel in Judges 6. When God directed him to gather the Israelite troops to defeat the Midianite invaders, Gideon wanted to be sure it was really God's voice he was hearing and that he understood

His directions. Gideon asked God for a sign to prove that this was truly His will. So he put out a piece of wool overnight an asked God to make it wet while keeping the surrounding dirt dry. God graciously did as Gideon asked, and in the morning the fleece was wet enough to produce a bowl of water when it was wrung out. But Gideon's faith was so weak that he asked God for another sign --- this tie to keep another fleece dry while making the surrounding dirt wet. Again, God complied and Gideon was finally convinced that God meant what He said. There are several lessons for us in Gideon's story. First, God is incredibly gracious and patient with us, especially when our faith is weak. Gideon knew he was treading on dangerous ground and was trying God's patience by asking for multiple signs.

God is a merciful, loving and patient God who knows our weaknesses. However, the story of Gideon should be for our instruction and not serve as a model for our own behavior. (story of Gideon taken from, GotQuestions?.Org.)

THE ALL INCLUSIVE CONDITION OF ANSWERED PRAYER

John 15:7, "If you abide in me, and my words abide in you, you shall ask what you will and it shall be done unto you."

The promise is "*ASK WHAT YOU WILL,*" plainly teaching that answered prayer is up to the child of God as to what he wants. Of course, whatever you are asking must be according to scripture and within God's will. It is in harmony with the promises of both testaments. A true Christian can get what he wants as well as what he needs. A "true Christian" is an obedient servant, in close relationship with God.

See the following scriptures for confirmation: Psalms 23:1, 34:9-10, 84:11; Matt 7:7-11, 17:20, 18:18-20, 21:22; Mark 9:23, 11:22-34; John 14:12-15, 16:23-26; Ephesians 3:20; Hebrews 11:6; James 1:5-8; 1John 3:21-22, 5:14-15.

A prayer saying: "IF it be Thy will" concerning anything God has already promised, and therefore has made it clear that it IS His will, providing we ask in faith, nothing wavering, is really a prayer of unbelief. It is like saying, "I know Lord, You have already promised and made it very clear by Your Word that it *IS* Your will, but do You really mean what You say? Are You a truthful God or not? Can we depend on what you say?" We insult God constantly questioning His will that is already revealed by His word. It is no less insulting to Him than it would be to a human friend who had promised something and we continue to question him about his will in the matter. Most likely he would respond by saying,"What is the matter with you? Have I not told you repeatedly that I would do it? Can you not take me at my word? Are you calling me a liar?" We would not do this to our friends as we trust their integrity. Then why would we do this to our heavenly Father who promised that He would do more for His children than any earthly parent?

James 4:2, "We have not because we ask not."

Some would argue, God knows what we need so why pray? He wants to hear from us, that's why. We were created for fellowship with God.

When I was in grade school, at the start of the year I would have to ask my Dad for book money. He knew he had to pay, but wanted me to ask him. It was a difficult task for me. I had to wait until he was in a good mood, which wasn't all the time! I was always afraid he might say no, but he never did. He always gave me the money.

By contrast, our heavenly Father is always in a good mood--always has what we need and is always available to listen.

I pray for wisdom to write the words/scriptures that will encourage you to pray. Not only for "big stuff" but for all things. 1 Thes 5:17, "Pray without ceasing."

PRAYER FOR THE LITTLE THINGS

The other day I got into a discussion with one of my Christian brothers. He felt he should not bother God with prayer for the "little things." As an example, looking for a parking place or green lights to arrive at your destination on time. I pray all the time for these kind of things! 1 Thes 5:17, "Pray without ceasing" and this, to me would be some reasons to stay in prayer all day long.

God made us for fellowship. To stay in close contact with Him daily we need to involve Him in our daily lives and the small things. Prov 16:3 "Commit your works unto the Lord and your thoughts shall be established." Take God into partnership and your plans will succeed. BEFORE doing anything--pray plan my day by keeping close to God for His wisdom, guidance and protection. If I happen to hit a closed door or speed bump, I stop and pray: "Father God, I prayed this morning for your help. What do I do now? Help me to make the right decision."

God is faithful. There may be a good reason He holds us up from an appointment. We may not see His plan for our day until later. One day when I was on my way to my weekly teaching, I had some stops to make. Whatever could go wrong, did. Now I was going to be late. When I prayed, God gave me a sense of peace and calm, and I knew it would be all right to be late that morning. Entering the parking lot, I ran into confrontation between the police and some people. The police had their guns drawn and loud, angry exchanges were in progress. As I got out of my car, I prayed for God to calm down all parties. At that moment, the campus pastor arrived and we stood in agreement for peace. In seconds, peace was restored! God had set up this divine appointment. He will do this for you also as He is no respecter of persons. You just need to remain in close relationship to God.

We do pray for larger things --- homes, cars, jobs, a Christian spouse. We better also be praying for salvation for our loved ones as well as others we know who need it.

Are we bothering God when we pray for the little things? Absolutely not!

Matthew 7:7-11, "Ask and it shall be given you; seek and you shall find; knock and it shall be opened unto you. For everyone that asks receives and he that seeks finds and to him who knocks it shall be opened. Or what man is there of you whom if his son asks for bread he will give him a rock? Or if he asks for a fish will he give him a serpent? If you then being evil, know how to give good gifts to your children, how much more shall your Father, who is in heaven, give good things to them that ask Him?"

If deliverance from dangers, preservation from evil, bodily healing and health, material prosperity or any other answer to prayer is a good thing, then ask to receive it and no longer question the will of God in the matter. It is already His will.

BE CAREFUL WHAT YOU PRAY FOR

You are responsible for what you pray for. We are to be good stewards with all we have as it explains in the parable of the unrighteous steward -- Luke:16. And we need to thank God for all we have, especially when He answers specific prayers for us. It is our nature to rejoice with what we have just received forgetting to give thanks and praise to our heavenly Father (from whom ALL good things come! James 1:17).

The enemy wants us to think we would have received even if we did not pray. Reality is God has already answered our prayers before we even ask, and we need to thank Him.

I remember a Thanksgiving turkey situation that occurred many years ago. My veterans group did a food drive every year for Thanksgiving and usually, enough had been donated to use for Christmas also. This one year, there was a shortage of turkeys. The fifth-graders at our local school faithfully did a food drive every year for our organization. After school, there was a meeting of this class to pray, asking for generous giving. Since it was an after school event, we were allowed to pray and so we did. We asked for God's provision and blessing as we still needed about 100 turkeys and other goods. When the day arrived that was the deadline for collecting the food and turkeys, the amount received was sparse. Then the truck, carrying the food donations from the school's collection arrived. I asked my fellow veterans if we received 100 turkeys. The answer was no, not 100 but 235!! Wow --- the Lord provided indeed!

Now a problem had developed as we had no where to keep the extra turkeys. One of our members had a connection at a local 7-11 store, however, and the 7-11 agreed to keep the extras in their freezer until the Christmas distribution. So, not only did God provide the food and turkeys, but also the place to store the fruit of His bounty. Hallelujah, Praise the Lord!

It is very easy to leave God out of the situation. We must make a habit of thanking Him for everything. God is in control. He is King of Kings and Lord of Lords. With Him there are no coincidences. He has plans for every believer: Jeremiah 29:11--- good and perfect plans before we were born!

It is discernment to know what is in the will of God and what is not. How do we know? Ask yourself if what you are requesting lines up with God's Word. If it does not, it is not His will but only your desire. God always knows best. If what we are asking for is not something we would be able to handle, God may say, "wait." If it would not be right or good for us, God may say "no." We have to trust Him and accept His will. He blesses us according to our needs, not wants and according to His purpose.

James 1:5, "But if any of you lacks wisdom, let him ask of God, who gives to all men generously and without reproach, and it will be given to him.'

HE THAT PRAYS TO GOD

Psalm 84: 5-12 (Word and commentary from NIV version)

84:5, *"How blessed are those whose strength is in you (God); who have set their hearts on pilgrimage."*

The pilgrimage to the temple passed through the barren valley of Baca. No specific valley has been identified with Baca.

Verse 6, *"As they pass through the valley of Baca, they make it a place of springs; the autumn rains also cover it with pools."*

Because Baca can mean "weeping," it may have been a symbolic reference to the times of struggles and tears through which people must pass on their way to meet God. Those who weep and seek God can be refreshed by rains and pools of spiritual water.

Verse 7, *"They go from strength to strength, till each appears before God in Zion."*

Growing strong in God's presence is often preceded by a journey through barren places in our lives.

Verse 8, *"Hear my prayer, O Lord God Almighty; listen to me O God of Jacob."*

The God of Jacob is addressed here for He met Jacob when Jacob was in distress and brought him out of his trouble. God met him when Jacob had nothing and God promised Jacob everything, thus becoming the God of all grace. God can do the same for others as He is no respecter of persons. In view of this truth, the psalmist gives forth more utterances of faith and benefit than requests to God. This is how it should be, for those who constantly beg God without faith and confidence in Him and His Word seldom receive much from God.

Verse 9, *"Look upon our shield, O God; look with favor on your anointed one."*

Verse 10, *"Better is one day in your courts than a thousand elsewhere; I would rather be a doorkeeper in the house of my God than dwell in the tents of the wicked."*

This is a characteristic of all children of God.

HE THAT TRUSTS IN GOD

Verse 11& 12, *"For the Lord is a sun and a shield; the Lord bestows favor and honor; no good thing does He withhold from those whose walk is blameless. O Lord Almigthy, blessed is the man who trusts in You."*

God does not promise to give us everything WE think is good, but He will not withhold what is permanently good. He will give us the means to walk along His paths, but we must do the walking. When we obey Him, He will not hold anything back that will serve Him.

PSALM 91 THE PRAYER THAT ANTICIPATES EVIL

Safety in Abiding in the Presence of God

Read Psalm 91.

Have you ever dialed 911 for an emergency? Many have. You can also call on God 24/7 with Psalm 91:1. "He who dwells in the secret place of the Most High shall abide under the shadow of the Almighty." We all need to declare daily: I (say your name) dwell in the secret place of the Most High and abide under the shadow of the Almighty. This is where I start and end my day as it is a comforting place to be. If God has you covered by His shadow, how can the enemy bother you? Luke 10:19 "I have given you authority to trample on snakes and scorpions and to overcome all the power of the enemy; **nothing will harm you.**" "Snakes and scorpions is symbolic for evil spirits. Snakes meaning the poison of lies and evils and scorpions meaning stings of hurts to our bodies, souls and spirits." Taken from a teaching by Nick Mellis.

Psalm 91:11, "For You, Father God, shall give Your angels charge over me in all my ways." What a wonderful thought!! Angels surrounding and guarding us ! How awesome is that? God loves us so much, He sends His angels to protect us.

Per Billy Graham: "The bible does tell us that for the believer nothing happens outside of God's control--and yes, if we know Christ, His angels continually watch over us. The bible says that God will command His angels concerning you to guard you in all your ways. It also teaches us that the angels, although they are largely unseen, watch over us and work for our good. Rather than only one angel, God surrounds us with a host of angels to protect us and go before us. Even when hard times come, Satan can never snatch us away from their protection--and someday, they will escort us safely to heaven." That is so awesome!

Are you "prayed up?" We need to be prepared as the best offense is a good defense, amen? The Boys Scouts motto is "always be prepared." This applies spiritually too.

Christians are aware of the enemy and the evil that abounds. We, as well as EVERYONE need God's protection. Man cannot fight the devil. He can only overcome through the power of God.

With The Lord's Prayer we ask God to "…deliver us from the evil one…" (Matt 6:13). Evil from the Greek: PENOS, literally means pain. It also denotes sin, sickness and poverty. These are absolutely things we want to avoid, amen?

The bible teaches that fallen angels are invisible, supernatural, angelic spirits created by God. Satan employs them as his immoral agents. After one-third of the heavenly angels sided with Satan, they were cast out of heaven to the earth. Rev. 12:4 While the bible doesn't offer the exact number of angels, the hosts could out number people. Of all the multitudes of angels God created, fallen angels comprise one-third. Satan keeps demons in bondage to his will, corrupting humans to separate from God. There are, however, many more of "God's good angels" than fallen ones. Logically, if Satan took one-third, there are still two thirds left, but the bible doesn't specifically give an amount.

On a separate page, there are many praise reports on the use of Psalm 91. There are many military praise reports. We are soldiers in Christ's army. We are Christian soldiers marching off into spiritual warfare on a daily basis. Prov 27:12, "The Prudent see danger and take refuge, but the simple keep going and suffer for it." Again in Hosea 4:6: " My people perish for lack of knowledge." Ignorance has been quoted as being "bliss" but it is no excuse to be ignorant of God's Word. When you do not prepare for the evil you may face, you leave a door open for Satan's attack. Pray Psalm 91 and the precious blood of Jesus over you and your family EVERY day!

The two most important things you do daily are prayer and reading God's Word. I pray for God to give me the words that are necessary to make you realize how important daily prayer and bible reading are in your life. There is nothing more important! When you start seeing results of both these practices, your faith will build and you will pray like never before. Hebrews 11 is the faith chapter. Without faith, it is impossible to please God. It is believed by many wise ones that the greater your understanding of the Gospel, the "Good News," (in the Greek the too good to be true news), the greater your faith will be. Romans 10:17 "Faith comes by hearing and hearing by the Word of God."

God waits to hear from you. He loves you and wants to spend time with you. Pray for God to increase your faith!

LIVING IN THE BALANCE OF GRACE AND FAITH

Taken from a teaching by Andrew Wommack

Ephesians 1:3

"Blessed is the God and Father of our Lord Jesus Christ, who has blessed us with every spiritual blessing in the heavenly places in Christ."

FAITH is resting in God's Amazing Grace, <u>*knowing*</u> (in your spirit) that God has already healed us and provided ALL things for us!

God has already blessed us with EVERY spiritual blessing-- everything you will ever need has been done, through Jesus, on the cross. Health, prosperity, joy, peace, love --EVERYthing is already DONE for you. Jesus said on the cross: **"It is finished."** Our part is to RECEIVE these promises by faith. ***<u>Do not doubt what you already have!!</u>***

When we are Born Again, ALL spiritual blessings are ours. We need to only receive all these blessings through faith in Him. We must ACT through agreement (faith.) Our faith only releases what God has already provided. No matter what illness or malady you have manifested in your flesh, ***Jesus has already healed it!*** BELIEVE AND RECEIVE THAT!

It is like a faucet. The water company has already provided all the water you need. All you have to do is turn on the tap! You can pray and pray and pray over that faucet. The water is already at your disposal, but you need to ACT (use your faith) and TURN ON THE TAP! Faith releases God's blessings.

Faith operates by the renewal of the mind, speaking His Word, and ***<u>receiving</u>*** what He has already provided. You have to believe (faith in action) ALL His promises are yes and amen! (2 Cor 1:20)

God's grace is independent of what you deserve—everything God does, He does by grace. Our part is to develop a faith that receives

His love and favor. God does not move in your life because of works: praying longer, going to church more often, helping others etc. He moves because of His Amazing Grace. God's Grace will only function according to the degree to which you respond. Grace is unearned and undeserved, but by faith you must discipline yourself and not engage in ungodly behavior and extremes.

So **_GRACE_** is God's part -----His Amazing Grace that has provided everything in Christ, and **_FAITH_** is our part in order to renew our minds and receive His blessings!!

HALLELUJAH!

DAILY HEALING PRAYER COVER
Based on writing of Joshua Ben and Theresa Melissa King

(Warning! This prayer is no religious ritual—Angels are programmed by God to carry it out as you pray it. Healing is real and you should expect results so pray with faith and energy!)

Heavenly Father, I pray this prayer in the power of the Holy Spirit and by the authority of the written Word of God and the victory of Jesus Christ, the anointed One, and by His blood and the Word in Luke 10:19:

As your servant, Lord Jesus, I take the keys of the Kingdom and exercise the power that has been give to me to tread upon serpents and scorpions and over all the power of the enemy. I declare that nothing shall by any means hurt me and...

In the mighty name of Jesus of Nazareth, I bind, rebuke, cast down and bring to no effect:

➤ *All powers, principalities, evil forces and all spiritual wickedness in this world that is against me, my family and those doing the work of God.*

➤ *All evil and generational curses and diseases, the powers of debt and lack, soul ties from sin and all filthy communication and negative words coming out of people's mouths.*

➤ *Everything standing in front of my total health, healing and restoration.*

➤ *All rejection, bitterness, rebellion and unforgiveness.*

➤ *All accusations, insecurity, passivity, depression, strife, control and retaliation.*

➢ *All sensitiveness, persecution, mental illness, paranoia, confusion, doubt, jealousy, withdrawal, escape, perfection, pride competition, judgmentalism, criticism and negative spirits.*

➢ *All pressure, impatience, over reaction, complacency, false burdens, grief, heaviness, worry, nervousness, stress, sexual impurities cults, death, selfishness and indecision.*

➢ *All self-deceptions, mind bindings, mind idolatries, fears of all types and unnatural affections.*

➢ *All fatigue, infirmity, disease, sickness, evil inheritances, hyper activities, cursing, addictive and compulsive behaviors.*

➢ *All gluttony, self-accusation, occult influence, witchcraft, religiousness, Spiritism, false religious beliefs, covetousness, guilt, shame and all other evil and unclean spirits.*

I loose myself from these forces in the name of Jesus Christ. I am God's property. I put the blood of Jesus Christ between these evil forces and me forever. No weapon, no evil shall prosper against me. (Isaiah 54:17 NKJV). I am submitted to God and I resist the devil so he will flee. (James 4:7). I take authority over this day so that it will be prosperous for my soul, body, mind, family, home, job, business dealings, finances and all that concerns me.

What does it mean to resist the devil, and why will resistance cause the devil to flee?

The phrase "resist the devil" is found in James 4:7 where the apostle James exhorts believers to resist the devil in order to cause him to flee or "run away" from us. To resist means to withstand, strive against, or oppose in some manner. Resistance can be a defensive maneuver on our part, such as resisting or withstanding the temptation to sin. Or it can be an action we take to use the only offensive weapon in the *full armor of God* (Ephesians 6:13-18), the sword of the spirit, which is the Word of God. Using the scriptures to expose Satan's lies and temptations is the most effective way to strive against and defeat them.

James 4:7, also says to "submit to God…" Resisting the devil must be accompanied by submitting to God. A disobedient believer will not see victory.

As Christians, we have full life when we are aware of the reality of the presence of evil. As we struggle to stand firm in our faith, we must realize that the enemies we are up against are not merely human ideas, but real forces that come from the powers of darkness. The Bible says: "For our struggle is not against flesh and blood, but against the rulers, against the powers, against the world forces of this darkness, against the spiritual forces of wickedness in the heavenly places." Eph 6:12.

Why will resistance cause the devil to flee? Because he knows he cannot have victory over us if we are prepared to do battle against him. The Bible assures us that we need only put on the full armor of God to be fully protected from evil and to actively resist it. There is nothing more frightening to satan than a believer who is fully equipped with spiritual armor!

I NOW LOOSE INTO MY LIFE TO ABOUND AND GROW:

Based on the scripture, Matthew 16:19

The fullness of the baptism of the Holy Spirit and fire. Holy Spirit, loose and stir up in me more words of wisdom, words of knowledge, faith, gifts of healings, workings of miracles, prophecy, discerning of spirits, tongues the interpretation of tongues. (Gifts of the Holy Spirit.)

Father, I pray for as your will be done, I will acknowledge and recognize it. I call forth my God-ordained destiny to materialize fully. Jeremiah 29:11, *"For I know the plans I have for you, declares the Lord, plans to prosper you and not to harm you, plans to give you a hope and a future."* I thank you that I stand firm in Your Spirit, centering in on the Gospel work.

I thank you, Father, that my family lives in harmony and unity, sharing the same love. We do nothing through strife and vain glory. We follow after righteousness, Godliness, faith, love, patience, meekness and longsuffering. Joshua 24:15, "…But for me and my household, we will serve the Lord."

Lord Jesus, I believe you died on the cross for my sins and rose from the dead. I am redeemed by Your blood and I belong to You. I confess all my sins known (name them) and unknown (Pray Holy Spirit reveals these to you). Lord Jesus, I renounce these sins. I forgive myself and everyone who has hurt me. I know, by Your Word, I am forgiven by my heavenly Father. Cleanse me now from all sin with Your precious blood.

GIVING GOD THE GLORY THROUGH HIS HOLY SPIRIT

Do you want to receive the *BAPTISM OF THE HOLY SPIRIT*?

A student once asked, "Do I have to get it? I am not sure that I want it!"

If you are thinking this way, there possibly is a spiritual battle going on. The enemy does not want Christians to receive the gift of tongues, as the Baptism of the Holy Spirit (and tongues) will bring you to a new level of spiritual awareness and raise you to a higher level of intercessory prayer. It is a level where you now become a threat to Satan and his dark kingdom.

There are reasons why some Christians do not receive the gift of tongues. God knows our heart and what we are capable of. He knows whom He can use spiritually. Those that qualify *will* receive His gift of tongues. There are those who are very weak. Weak Christians are not fully committed. They do not read their Bible on a regular basis or pray much---except when they have an urgent need. Generally, they are those who do not fully trust God and His promises---full of fears, anxiety and doubt.

"Fence sitters" or those living in sin, will most likely not receive this gift, as they are ineffective and therefore would be dangerous in the spiritual realm. Fence sitters are termed "Lukewarm Christians" in the Bible. Rev 3:14-22; 1John 2:15-16 (as well as many other reference verses in the Bible.) They have one foot in the spiritual and one foot still in the world. They are totally ineffective.

You can pray to receive the Baptism of the Holy Spirit for God's glory. Although it is an excellent "tool" we also want it to glorify our Father. James 1:17, "Every good and perfect gift is from above, coming down from the Father of lights, who does not change like shifting shadows." Any gift we are blessed with from God needs to be shared--not hidden. Luke 11:33: "No one lights a lamp and puts it in a place where it will be hidden…"

The parable of the talents, Matthew 25:14-30 is generally thought to have been about money, however, I have heard teachings on this as being your gifts or talents---not money.

Romans 11:29 NIV: "For God's gifts and His call are irrevocable." the NKJ says: "for the gifts and calling of God are without repentance." This means we are required to function in the gifts God gives us, using them for God's glory. If we mess up, God will be patient and give us other chances.

Usually, when we first receive the gift of tongues we are perplexed. We wonder if this is authentic--- if we did receive this gift or are we just uttering gibberish? There even may be a feeling of anxiety or fear concerning authenticity. But the Holy Spirit will give us blessed assurance and confirmation that this indeed is very real and a beautiful gift from God Almighty! How awesome this truly is! As we mature and grow in our faith and journey with the Lord, we will become powerful prayer warriors equipped with the full armor of God, Eph 6:13-17, and the power of His Holy Spirit. Hallelujah!

Another obstacle could be a former teaching. Baptists, for instance, do not speak in tongues, as they believe this was Old Testament and no longer functions. There may be other denominations that do not embrace this gift. If you have grown up with this kind of teaching, it will be difficult to unlearn and relearn, but if God wants you to have the gift of tongues, you will receive it. Remember, the devil does not want you to speak in tongues. He only wants you in bondage and believing his lies--he wants you to remain weak and ineffective.

My own personal experience was at first I prayed and prayed and prayed. Then one day I opened my mouth and realized I was speaking in tongues! It was amazing.

My wife and I pray for others on a regular basis, and we are always cautious that we do not upset or frighten someone who is either not familiar with, or does not believe in speaking in tongues. They still need the prayer and we do not want to intimidate them. Generally, we will pray in tongues silently. I will pray out loud for that person while my wife silently prays in tongues or vice versa. The person is receiving the benefit of Holy Spirit power and it works very well. We do receive many praise reports! Praise God!

Here is a short story that will amaze you --- nothing is impossible for God!! I once ministered with a young man who received the Baptism of the Holy Spirit during a drug deal!! It scared him into repentance! He is now on a mission to get his credentials to become a pastor! Don't we serve an extraordinary God? Amen!

I pray you will receive the Baptism of the Holy Spirit and be used greatly in God's plan.

FOUR CONDITIONS FOR RECEIVING THE BAPTISM OF THE HOLY SPIRIT

1. **Thirst.** John 7:37-39, "On the last and greatest day of the Feast, Jesus stood and said in a loud voice, *"If anyone is thirsty, let him come to me and drink. Whoever believes in me , as the scripture has said, streams of living water will flow from within him."* By this he meant the Spirit, whom those who believed in Him were later to receive. Up to that time the Spirit had not been given, since Jesus had not yet been glorified." As per commentary from NIV of the Bible: " Jesus' words, *"come to me and drink"* alluded to the theme of many Bible passages that talk about the Messiah's life-giving blessings(Isaiah 12:2-3, 44:3-4, 58:11). In promising to give the Holy Spirit to all who believed, Jesus was claiming to be the Messiah, for that was something only the Messiah could do. Jesus used the term *living water* in John 4:10 to indicate eternal life. Here He uses the term to refer to the Holy Spirit. The two go together. Thirst indicates, therefore, the ardent, eager, famishing, keen and all consuming craving and passion of the soul for complete union with God and the fullness of the Spirit. Ps 42:2-3, "As the deer pants for streams of water, so my soul pants for you, O God. My soul thirsts for God, for the living God. When can I go and meet with God?"

2. **Come unto me.** Matt 11:28, *"Come to me, all you who are weary and burdened and I will give you rest."* This means the complete surrender of the life to do the whole will of God as light is received. It means casting all your cares on Jesus. Ps 55:22 *"Cast your cares on the Lord and He will sustain you. He will never let the righteous fall."* Jesus frees people from burdens.

3. **Drink.** (John 7:37) This means the whole-hearted reception into one's life of the gifts, the fruit and the operations of the Holy Spirit. 1 Cor 12:4-13.

4. **<u>Believe in Me.</u>** John 7:38, This means to believe in and obey completely, the whole Gospel.

   Verse 37 is a prophecy from God.

   Verses 38 and 39 are promises from God.

   Once you receive the Baptism of the Holy Spirit, and receive the gift of tongues, or what is also know as "your heavenly language or prayer language," you will wonder how you were able to pray as effectively without it! Your prayer life will expand to an extent you cannot imagine!

   I want to make a note here. There ARE believers, who are indeed filled with the Holy Spirit, that have not received the gift of tongues. Tongues are NOT what gets you to heaven! They are a manifestation of the *Baptism* of the Holy Spirit, but not everyone gets this gift. God will give tongues to those He chooses, and we do not question His wisdom!

   The Apostle Paul did not say that spiritual gifts were an option and that a believer was free to accept or reject them as is commonly believed in some circles. The spiritual gifts did not disappear with the original apostles. They are to be part of the normal, ordinary Christian experience. Believers are not to be passive, indifferent, neutral or unbelieving concerning the gifts, but instead, they are to desire them strongly and to be open to receiving them from God. 1 Cor 14:1, "Follow the way of love and eagerly desire spiritual gifts…"

   The first and most important use of tongues is to pray for yourself! We need to cover ourselves in prayer daily to get us through the day. You may not know what to pray for on that particular day, but the Holy Spirit knows what you need and praying in tongues accesses His power to cover you completely.

   Paul prayed almost exclusively in tongues. If <u>he</u> found it necessary to pray in tongues often to build himself up spiritually, we as modern believers should do the same.

Here we are addressing tongues for intercession. What better way to pray for family, friends, and others, whom we do not know their hearts, than to pray in tongues, allowing the Holy Spirit to connect with their spirit. My wife, Janet and I are on the altar prayer team at our church. Many times someone will come forward for prayer, but is unwilling to divulge their need. Praying for them in tongues covers whatever is not spoken. There are also those who will share one thing they want prayer for, but omit other, more important requests for reasons known only to them. Tongues covers all. Nothing is omitted. This is why is it one of the "gifts" and it is a powerful tool.

INTERCESSION IN TONGUES

Romans 8:26-27, "In the same way, the Spirit helps us in our weakness. We do not know what we ought to pray for, but the Spirit Himself intercedes for us with groans that words cannot express. And He who searches our hearts knows the mind of the Spirit, because the Spirit intercedes for the saints in accordance with God's will."

This is the work of the Divine Trinity in believers, the Holy Spirit's work. We are temples of the Holy Spirit. He dwells in us from the moment we are born again. His presence enables us to intercede, as God would have us pray. This is closely similar to the benefits and differences between a cell or smart phone and a landline. I was a hold out to get first a cell and then a smart phone and now that I have one, I cannot believe how convenient it is to have such a technology at my fingertips! This is like the gift of tongues----once you get it, you wonder how you prayed as effectively without it.

Again, I must iterate, in Luke 3:16, NKJ, John the Baptist is talking: "John answered saying to all "I indeed baptize you with water, but One mightier than I is coming, whose sandal strap I am not worthy to loose. He will baptize you with the Holy Spirit and fire." The commentary on this scripture explains: "John the Baptist told of Jesus Christ who would baptize the people with the Holy Spirit and fire. The Bible teaches the reality of and the need for *the baptism of the Holy Spirit, which is a complete immersion in the Spirit of God, by which a persons motivations are set on fire by the power of God*. When a person receives the baptism of the Holy Spirit, he receives supernatural power to live and witness for God. (Acts 1:8)." 2 Cor 1:22, "...(God) who has sealed us and given us the Spirit in our hearts as a **guarantee**." The Holy Spirit living is us is God's guarantee that we will live forever with Him in heaven and that He will complete the work He has started in us. God is not asking us to trust Him on blind faith. He has given us the Holy Spirit as a deposit or a pledge that He means what He says."

Tongues is a gift---and it is a visible manifestation of the Baptism of the Holy Spirit, but not everyone receives this gift. That does NOT mean a believer is not filled with the power of the Holy Spirit.

Acts 20:27, "For I have not shunned to declare to you the whole counsel of God."

As explained in commentary from NKJ: "Paul declared the whole counsel of God to God's people. He did not go off on a tangent or emphasize one truth to the exclusion of others. The 'whole counsel of God' refers to the larger picture of God's plan. Spiritual deception or diminishing fullness of experience and ministry by the body of Christ often begins when men and women preach only part of the counsel of God. Believers in Christ should be familiar with the entire Bible and not just certain passages."

I, personally, thank God that I am gifted with tongues as I am a prayer warrior and tongues has been and is an unbelievable asset to the effectiveness of my prayers.

THE BENEFITS OF TONGUES

Taken from a paper written by Pastor Tom Hoffman, Grace and Peace Church, Toms River, NJ:

Brain specialist Dr. Carl Peterson of Oral Roberts University, Tulsa Oklahoma, has uncovered some interesting evidence regarding the power of God through our prayer and worship in the Spirit.

As a result of his research, Dr. Peterson has discovered that as we pray in the Spirit, a brain activity begins to take place that would not otherwise occur. He has found that as we pray and worship in tongues, the brain releases two chemical secretions that are directed into our immune system giving a 35 to 40 percent boost to the immune system. He also states that this secretion is triggered by a part of the brain that has no other apparent activity in humans! Our Spirit-led prayer and worship only activate it.

Let's tap into this reservoir of life that God has placed in us. Praying in the spirit is not a religious act, but a direct connection with the Spirit of the Lord that is a benefit to us all for the glory of God. This gave me a deeper appreciation of the body being a temple of the Holy Spirit. 1 Cor 6:19.

As you go before the Lord in prayer, consider this information and revel in the magnitude of the following scripture: 1 John 4:4 "You are of God, little children, and have overcome them because He who is in you is greater than he who is in the world. (NKJV)

LET US ALL WORSHIP GOD IN SPIRIT AND IN TRUTH AND RECEIVE THE PROMISES OF GOD.

READING THE BIBLE

Part of our daily bread is reading the Bible daily. This is not optional for any Christian--we need Bible reading to get us through the day.

How to start? You do not read it like a novel. You can, but it is not what is recommended. There are many guides on how to read the Bible. Some Bibles even have the recommended reading incorporated. You can also pick up such a guide at any Christian bookstore.

If this is your first time reading the Bible, or your first actual "in depth" study, the Bible differs from anything else you'll ever study. Penned by inspiration of God Himself in perfectly timed progressive revelation over hundreds of years and sixty-six books by 40 authors, it is far more than history or literature. It is a divinely inspired meeting place where God reveals Himself and invites us into relationship.

Go to the New Testament to the Gospels, Matthew, Mark, Luke and John. Do not start with Matthew -- go to John. Although it was the last written, John is the easiest to understand (and it's the "warm and fuzzy" gospel). John was 95 when he wrote it. He was part of the inner circle very close to Jesus. (The inner circle was comprised of Peter, Andrew, John and James.) John also wrote John 1, 2 and 3 and Revelation.

Then go back and read the other Gospels. Psalms and Proverbs can be added, one or two a day if desired. Note: I would highly recommend, for the new believer especially, getting the Life Application Study Bible, New International Version (NIV) as this version is easy to understand and has abundant commentary explaining scripture. Then read the rest of the New Testament when you are on your own. When you are comfortable with it, it is time to read it.

Scripture cannot come without effect to the receptive soul. Isaiah 55:11 tells us, "My Word will not come back void." God's Word is living, healing, restoring, enlightening, directing and empowering. It invades every part of our lives if we will let it. You will never waste a moment you spend with an open heart in God's Word.

The Bible says it, I believe it, that settles it! A best seller every year, published in over 2,460 languages and 6 versions in brail. It is banned in certain countries and it's possession is punishable by death. Every time someone has tried to destroy it, it has come back stronger!

Key scripture 2 Timothy 3:16-17, "All scripture is God breathed and is useful for teaching, rebuking, correcting and training in righteousness, so that the man of God may be thoroughly equipped for every good work."

Read the Bible slowly, frequently, prayerfully, meditatively, searchingly and devotionally and study it constantly. It will change you. It will enrich your life and influence your thoughts and actions. It will make you a better you!

The Bible is a mine of wealth, a source of health and a world of pleasure. It is the wisdom, will and heart of Almighty God. ALL your answers are in that book.

Personalize it:

This is MY Bible.
I am what it says I am.
I have what it says I have.
I can do what it says I can do.
God will do what He promises He will do.
ALL God's promises are yes and amen.
Today I will be taught by the Word of God,
I boldly confess my mind is alert,
My heart is receptive
And I will never be the same again.
In Jesus' Name

The following is an interesting perspective on reading the bible:

THE STORY IS TOLD OF AN OLD MAN WHO LIVED ON A FARM IN THE MOUNTAINS OF KENTUCKY WITH HIS YOUNG GRANDSON. EACH MORNING, GRANDPA WAS UP EARLY SITTING AT THE KITCHEN TABLE READING FROM HIS OLD, WORN-OUT BIBLE. HIS GRANDSON, WHO WANTED TO BE JUST LIKE HIM TRIED TO IMITATE HIM IN ANY WAY HE COULD.

ONE DAY THE GRANDSON ASKED, 'GRAMPA, I TRY TO READ THE BIBLE JUST LIKE YOU BUT I DON'T

UNDERSTAND IT, AND WHAT I DO UNDERSTAND

I FORGET AS SOON AS I CLOSE THE BOOK.

WHAT GOOD DOES READING THE BIBLE DO?

THE GRANDFATHER QUIETLY TURNED FROM PUTTING COAL IN THE STOVE AND SAID:

TAKE THIS COAL BASKET DOWN TO THE RIVER AND

BRING BACK A BASKET OF WATER.

THE BOY DID AS HE WAS TOLD, EVEN THOUGH

ALL THE WATER LEAKED OUT BEFORE HE COULD

GET BACK TO THE HOUSE.

THE GRANDFATHER LAUGHED AND SAID,

"YOU WILL HAVE TO MOVE A LITTLE FASTER

NEXT TIME." HE THEN SENT HIM BACK TO THE RIVER WITH THE BASKET TO TRY AGAIN.

THIS TIME THE BOY RAN FASTER, BUT AGAIN THE

BASKET WAS EMPTY BEFORE HE RETURNED HOME.
OUT OF BREATH, HE TOLD HIS GRANDFATHER
IT IS IMPOSSIBLE TO CARRY WATER IN A
BASKET AND WENT TO GET A BUCKET INSTEAD.

THE OLD MAN SAID, "I DON'T WANT A BUCKET OF
WATER, I WANT A BASKET OF WATER.
YOU MUST TRY HARDER. AT THIS POINT THE BOY
KNEW IT WAS IMPOSSIBLE BUT HE WANTED TO SHOW HIS
GRANDFATHER THAT EVEN IF HE RAN AS FAST AS HE COULD
THE WATER WOULD LEAK OUT.

IN EXASPERATION AND OUT OF BREATH HE SAID
"SEE GRANDPA, IT'S USELESS!"

"SO YOU THINK IT'S USELESS?" THE OLD MAN SAID--
"LOOK AT THE BASKET."

THE BOY LOOKED AND FOR THE FIRST TIME
HE REALIZED THAT THE BASKET LOOKED DIFFERENT.
INSTEAD OF A DIRTY OLD COAL BASKET,
IT WAS CLEAN.

"SON, THAT'S WHAT HAPPENS WHEN YOU READ THE
BIBLE. YOU MIGHT NOT UNDERSTAND OR REMEMBER
EVERYTHING, BUT WHEN YOU READ IT,

IT WILL CHANGE YOU FROM THE INSIDE OUT."

THAT IS THE WORK OF GOD IN OUR LIVES.

TO CHANGE US FROM THE INSIDE OUT AND

TO SLOWLY TRANSFORM US INTO THE IMAGE OF HIS SON!

THINK ABOUT IT

Chaplain Tom Conti

ABIDING AND CONFIDING

I am crucified with Jesus, and He lives and dwells with me; I have ceased from all my struggling 'Tis no longer I, but He. All my will is yielding to Him and His Spirit reigns within; And His precious blood each moment keeps me cleansed and free from sin.

All my sickness I bring to Him, and he bears them all away; All my fears and grief I tell Him, all my cares from day to day. All my strength I draw from Jesus, by his breath I live and move; Even His very mind He gives me, and His faith and life and love. For my words I take His wisdom, for my works His Spirit's power; for my ways His ceaseless presence guards and guides me every hour. Of my heart He is the portion, of my joy the boundless spring; Savior, Sanctifier, Healer, Glorious Lord and coming King!

Taken from "The Gospel of Healing"

By A.B. Simpson

THE FIELD CROSS

Chaplains Listening Post—January, 2004
Written by: Rev Tom Conti
Chaplain, Vietnam Brotherhood
B Company

What is a field cross? A field cross is a rifle with a fixed bayonet stuck in the ground, having a helmet on the rifle butt, combat boots alongside and dog tags hanging off the rifle.

I saw a field cross-tattooed on a man's leg. Thinking he was a Vet, I commented on the cross. To my surprise, he was not a Vet, but his father was a Vietnam Veteran. Wow--what a tribute! Some sons spend most of their lives trying to please their fathers and never do.

The first time I saw a field cross was in country, Vietnam--Nov. 1966. My unit was at a formation on our base camp. In front of us were about 12 field crosses. I remember the names and ranks being called off in solemn tribute to our fallen brothers. I did not know any of them. It was an ominous moment realizing the next time it could be *your* name being called.

Years later, as a member of V.V.A. Chapter 200 in N.J., we would march in big parades a couple of times a year. Our tradition while waiting to step off in the order of march would be to find a bagpiper. Our color guard formed a circle. One of us would fix a bayonet on his rifle, put his helmet on it and stick it in the center of the circle. We were then called to attention. With the flags flying, and a large crowd forming, the bagpiper would play "Amazing Grace." A very poignant moment with silence, tears and mixed emotions. Today, whenever I hear the pipes, I get choked up again.

As contrast to our earthly fathers, our heavenly Father is a lot easier to please. He does not expect us to get tattooed or bend over backward trying to please Him. He just wants us to spend time with Him. That is called prayer accompanied by a thank you to God, that a field cross does not have our dog tags on it as we are not yet finished with His plan for us.

THE DIFFERENCE

I got up early one morning and rushed right into the day...
I had so much to accomplish, I didn't have time to pray.

Problems just tumbled about me--and heavier came each task...
"Why doesn't God help me?" I wondered...
He said "But you didn't ask."

I wanted to see joy and beauty but the day toile on gray and bleak...
I wondered why God didn't show me?
He said "But you didn't seek."

I tried to come into God's presence--I used all my keys at the lock...
God gently and lovingly chided: "My child, you didn't knock."

I woke up early this morning and paused before entering the day.
I had so much to accomplish --- that I had to take time to pray!

UNANSWERED PRAYER

Why are some prayers answered and some not? There have been many books written on this topic, many sermons preached, and many teachings taught. The truth of this matter is God does answer prayer--- it just may not be what you were expecting, like or even recognize. We must understand that God's answer could be "no," which can be difficult to deal with or accept. Isaiah 55:8-9, "For my thoughts are not your thoughts, neither are your ways my ways. For as the heavens are higher than the earth, so are My ways higher than your ways." As Christians, we have to understand that God is always right, and there are reasons you don't always get what you want or pray for. Trust in God!

God is sovereign and He is in control. None of our prayers are wasted, though sometimes this seems to be the case. In your quiet time, ask God why your prayers are not being answered in a way you can understand and recognize, then quiet yourself and wait on Him. He may answer you through scripture, through a sermon you hear that you recognize as a "word in season," through another brother or sister in Christ, or just directly through your spirit. Always read your bible, as the Word is alive and can speak to your heart.

The enemy of our soul does not want us to pray. Satan is the father of lies, and he will try to convince you it is of no use to pray. He will also use tactics to keep you from praying like distractions that take up the time you could have spent with the Lord. Do not listen to such lies from hell, and be sure to keep praying on a daily basis. Prayer changes things! Our prayers enhance our relationship with God and we receive strength from Him. This is why the enemy does not want us to pray---it strengthens us and weakens him!

As children, we ask and pray for whatever we want. We learn fast that unreasonable requests will not be fulfilled. As adults, some have not yet learned foolish requests will not be honored. I have been asked to pray for someone to win the lottery! I just laughed and told them to put their lottery money in the church collection marked "missions." That will bless them far more than winning the lottery.

Some people will use unanswered prayer as an excuse for their no longer praying. They are treading into dangerous territory, as the enemy will seize the opportunity to darken their mind and prevent God's blessings from flowing into their life. Never stop praying! It is not only pleasing to God to hear your prayers, but it provides you with protection and other blessings. Remember, the enemy is a liar---do NOT listen to him.

Your prayers must always be in line with what scripture says. Find some scriptures that line up with your prayer request, then memorize them and be able to quote chapter and verse. God's Word does not come back void! (Isaiah 55:11).

SCRIPTURES ON UNANSWERED PRAYER

Proverbs 28:9 (NIV,) *"If anyone turns a deaf ear to the law, even his prayers are detestable."*

From NIV commentary: "God does not listen to our prayers if we intend to go back to our sin as soon as we get off our knees. If we want to forsake our sin and follow Him, however, He willingly listens--no matter how bad our sin *has been*. What closes His ears is not the depth of our sin, but our secret intention to do it again. God hears our intentions as clearly as He hears our words."

The following scriptures address unanswered prayer:

1. Refusing to hear the truth................ Proverbs 28:9
2. Refusing to humble self...................2 Chronicles 7:14
3. Forsaking God .... 2 Chronicles 15:2
4. Provoking God...........................Deuteronomy 3:26
5. Hard-heartedness....................... Zechariah 7:12-13
6. Lack of charity.......................... Proverbs 21:13
7. Regarding iniquity in heart............. Psalm 66:18
8. Wrong motives.......................... James 4:3
9. Dishonor of companion................ 1 Peter 3:7
10. Unbelief.................................... Matthew 17:20 and 21:22
11. Sin... James 4:1-5; John 9:31; Isaiah 59:3
12. Parading prayer life.................... Matthew 6:5
13. Vain repetitions........................ Matthew 6:7

14. Unforgiveness.......................... Matthew 6:14-15 and
Mark 11:25-26

15. Hypocrisy............................... Luke 18:9-14

16. Being discouraged....................... Luke 18:1-8

17. Worry and anxiety....................... Philippians 4:6

18. Doubting and double mindedness...... James 1:5-8

Also see Proverbs 3:32: "Abominations"

Page 643 of the Dake Bible offers 20 things that are an abomination to God.

THE UNRIVALED POWER OF PRAYER
Taken from Oswald Chambers daily devotional, November 8

Romans 8:26, *"We know not what we should pray for as we ought, but the Spirit Himself makes intercession for us with groanings which cannot be uttered."*

"We realize that we are energized by the Holy Spirit for prayer and we know what it is to pray in accordance with the Spirit, but we don't often realize that the Holy Spirit Himself prays prayers in us which we cannot utter ourselves. When we are born again of God and are indwelt by the Spirit of God, He expresses for us the unutterable.

"He," the Holy Spirit in you, "makes intercession for the saints according to the will of God." (Romans 8:27). And God searches your heart, not to know what your conscious prayers are, but to find out what the prayer of the Holy Spirit is.

The spirit of God uses the nature of the believer as a temple in which to offer His prayers of intercession. "...your body is the temple of the Holy Spirit..." (1 Corinthians 6:19).

When Jesus Christ cleansed the temple, "...He would not allow anyone to carry wares through the temple" (Mark 11:16). The Spirit of God will not allow you to use your body for your own convenience. Jesus ruthlessly cast out everyone who bought and sold in the temple, and said: "My house shall be called a house of prayer...but you have made it a den of thieves" (Mark 11:17).

Have we come to realize that our "body is the temple of the Holy Spirit?" If so, we must be careful to keep it undefiled for Him. We have to remember that our conscious life, even though only a small part of our total person, is to be regarded by us as a "temple of the Holy Spirit." He will be responsible for the unconscious part which we don't know, but we must pay careful attention to and guard the conscious part for which we are responsible.

Romans 8:28 (NIV)

"And we know that in all things God works for the good of those who love Him, who have been the called according to His purpose."

God ordains the circumstances of a saint's life. In the life of a saint, there is no such thing as chance. God, by His providence, brings you into circumstances that you may not understand, but the Holy Spirit of God understands and is there to guide and council you.

God gives us divine appointments on a regular basis. We must be ever alert to this so we do not miss the opportunity to help and/or pray for others. God sends people to us and expects us to reach out and help, even if it is inconvenient or uncomfortable for us. God knows we are capable, that's why He sends those He does and we must recognize our responsibility as Christians. This is being a good witness as well as helping someone in need. Most of us have missed opportunities largely because we were not alert to the calling. It then comes as a revelation that we missed it, and should prepare us to be more responsive the next time. I have missed opportunities and have been very upset but determined to be more aware the next time as it is a sad thing to miss what God has sent. It happens, but again, we need to be always more responsive so we don't miss it!

There are also occasions where we are only called to prayer. This is the heart of intercession and usually tongues are used as we don't always know why we are praying for someone---we just know we need to pray for them. The Holy Spirit knows and when we pray in tongues, we are praying as the Holy Spirit would have us pray. This is beyond anything we can comprehend, but without such intercession, someone would be impoverished spiritually.

Prayer works---- prayer changes US so we can be more useful to God! Prayer brings Glory to God, and peace to us.

THE UNPARDONABLE SIN

Reference: NKJ Spirit Filled Life Bible for Students, pg 1218

Matthew 12:31:

"Therefore I say to you, every sin and blasphemy will be forgiven men, but the blasphemy against the Spirit will not be forgiven men."

"The concept of an unpardonable sin has been a source of difficulty for many because it seems to go against the Bible's teaching about grace. We understand that God's grace forgives every sin, but our Lord mentioned one sin that cannot be forgiven.

The religious leaders had come out to hear Him, but they opposed virtually everything He said. As He was casting out demons, they accused Him of doing this by satanic means. (Matt:12:24).

Obviously, the unpardonable sin is not merely saying an unkind thing about the Holy Spirit, the religious leaders involved had turned totally against the revelation of God. They were so far into their own wickedness that they rejected not only Jesus Christ, but also the Holy Spirit. They were saying that good was evil and evil was good. They called the Spirit of God Satan!

Once they had rejected Jesus, the one source of forgiveness, there was now no forgiveness. A person who turns away from Jesus Christ can receive no forgiveness, and that is what these had done.

If you want to obey God but are concerned that you have committed the unpardonable sin, you have NOT committed it. If anyone today has committed this sin, it would be one who is hard-hearted, who has turned against Jesus, reviled Him and become so depraved that he would claim that God's Spirit is Satan."

MORE UNPARDONABLE SIN

There are people who Satan has completely blinded and they have bought into his lies. Their lives are full of bad things and depravity. They are the lost. If any among them regards God as satanically motivated, they have committed the unpardonable sin. Some even worship the devil. For people to turn against God in such an abominable manner there had to be circumstances in their lives to influence such unbelief in the only one who could help them? It's a very sad situation.

Some years ago, for a season, my wife, Janet and I had volunteered on a 1-800 prayer line. We did this through the church we were then attending. Prayer requests came in from every state. We were amazed at how many callers truly believed they had committed the unpardonable sin. Guilt from their past had engineered feelings of hopelessness and unworthiness and they simply felt they could not be forgiven and therefore had committed the unpardonable sin. They had stopped praying because of feelings of futility and that their prayers did not count. Can you recognize the actions of the enemy in all this? Satan used their circumstances to try to wrench them away from God, and stop their prayers.

However, the fact that these poor souls were calling a prayer line indicates the Holy Spirit still had a handle on their destiny! Praise God! We shared that fact with them and assured them that God still loved them and they did NOT commit the unpardonable sin. We then suggested they find a bible believing church and seek some council. I must say, most of them were encouraged and relieved and I feel in my heart, the Holy Spirit was at work in their hearts as we prayed with them, and He had inspired the phone call! Hallelujah!

For over a year, I ministered to a young man who was hung up on the unpardonable sin issue. He had worshipped at the church of Satan for a season and his guilt was extreme. His entire family was still into devil worship, which, of course, did not help matters. He had been in and out of prison and was obviously a very troubled individual. In his case, it is difficult to determine where he really is in his heart because of former devil worship. I lost contact with him as he moved away.

One day a young woman entered the Sunday School class we were attending. This was her first time at class. When class ended, she came up for prayer. She was trembling and appeared to be in great distress. Some of us laid hands on her and prayed. God's Holy Spirit prompted us to ask is she was saved. She answered "yes." There is a form of confirmation for someone who claims to be saved or to be Christian. You request they say. "Jesus Christ is my Lord and Savior." She had great difficulty saying these words. After several attempts and much anxiety, she finally was able to blurt out and say, "Jesus Christ is my Lord and Savior!" We all rejoiced! Obviously, she had an oppression that was overcome. We never saw her again.

Romans 10:9-10, *"That if you shall confess with your mouth that Jesus Christ is your Lord and Savior and shall believe in your heart that God raised Him from the dead, you shall be saved. For with the heart man believes unto righteousness and with the mouth confession is made unto salvation."*

The enemy would like us all to think we have committed the unpardonable sin. He does not want us to pray, read the bible or go to church. When he reminds us of our past, we need to rebuke him in the name of Jesus and remind him of his future! We Christians know the ending of the book---Satan and all his followers will burn in the lake of fire. Revelation 19:20.

We all need to thank Jesus Christ for being our Lord and Savior. He died that we may live. Jesus is Lord ----

WHY ARE NOT ALL THE SICK HEALED?

We do not have all the answers. I am often asked why am I not healed. My answer is you must ask God, who is the only one who holds all knowledge and truth. Some insist they do not hear from God so I reply: have you read your bible today? God speaks through His Word directly to your heart.

God is sovereign and He can do whatever He wants to do. Divine healing was provided at Calvary. Jesus died for our sins and our healing. For those who do not experience the healing they pray for, God is a good God and only He has the answer. You must trust in Him and not give up. His will is that we do obey His Word and commands. Reward for this is blessings. It is so important to understand, God will not go against anyone's free will. But He does have biblical guidelines He expects His people to follow and obey. If, by your own free choice, you decide to live outside of His Word and live a sinful lifestyle, you cannot expect God to ignore that! He is good and He is *just.* Examine your own choices and lifestyle. Are you living in His will? God cannot contradict His own Word and instructions. He loves all of us, but we limit His moving in our favor by our choices and decisions.

Some people believe (have the misconception) that God wants them to be sick. Like Paul who had the thorn in his side and couldn't get rid of it. This is just not true. It is a lie from the pit of hell meant to discourage those who are suffering and cause them lack of faith.

Hosea 4:6 "My people perish for lack of knowledge." The enemy of our soul does not want us to know the truth and uses times of suffering to enforce his lies. God does not want anyone to be sick.

When Kenneth Hagan Sr. was a teenager, he had been given a literal death sentence. His Methodist Pastor asked him what songs he would like sung at his funeral, for Kenneth was to die any day. Hearing this made him very angry and he went to his bible to find contradictory verses. He found Isaiah 53:4-5, "By Jesus's stripes we are healed." Kenneth Hagan Senior, served the Lord for over 70 years before going home as he trusted in God and believed His Word.

None of us knows the power the Word has for us. We have not studied scripture long enough, but remaining faithful to reading the bible is essential for our spiritual growth and understanding. God does have a plan and a future for every one of us as it says in Jeremiah 29:11. The heart of the verse is not that we would escape our lot, but that we would learn to thrive in the midst of it.

If you are a born again believer, your body is the temple of the Holy Spirit. Be careful what you do with and to it! You need to live both physically and spiritually healthy. Ps 139:14, "I will praise You (the Lord) for I am fearfully and wonderfully made." However, if you abuse your body, you will reap consequences. Tobacco, alcohol, drugs, unhealthy (processed and fast) foods, too much sugar, not enough sleep, over eating, lack of exercise all harm our physical bodies just as lack of prayer and the Word harm us spiritually. Prayer is of utmost urgency to keep our bodies healthy as prayer heals. Prayer is heard by our Father in heaven and thus can move His hand. Prayer comforts us and conquers fear because it brings us into God's presence. Unhealthy people need to look at and address their lifestyle choices! Learn to read labels--- if you can't pronounce it, don't ingest it! Lose excess weight, as it is harmful to your body. Here again, pray about this and God will help you make the proper choices. Remember, the older you get, the more you need to take care of your body! Don't expect miracles when you are not doing your part. This goes for the physical care and the spiritual!

My prayer for you is to take control of your own health. Treat your body as the temple of the Holy Spirit and don't expose it to bad choices. You will feel so much better and be more productive.

SPIRITUAL WARFARE
OF ALL BELIEVERS

Put on the Amour of God—Ephesians 6:10-20

Paul wrote the letter of Ephesians not only to the believers in the church of Ephesus, but to all believers.

Many years ago, I took a course where one of the exercises was to read the book of Ephesians three times a day for thirty days. I was less than excited about this exercise because I wanted to finish this part of the teaching and move on to the next. At some point I realized what a great book Ephesians is, not only for 64 AD but for today! I now go daily to this book, as there are so many "pearls" in it. I recommend you read the entire book slowly and reverently as it will surely improve your life. Please note Ephesians 3:14-21, which provides prayers for the full blessings of God. These are powerful verses:

"For this reason I kneel before the Father, from whom His whole family in heaven and on earth derives its name. I pray that out of His glorious riches He may strengthen you with power through His spirit in your inner being, so that Christ may dwell in your hearts through faith. And I pray that you, being rooted and established in love, may have power together with all the saints, to grasp how wide and long and high and deep is the love of Christ, and to know His love that surpasses knowledge--that you may be filled to the measure of all the fullness of God. Now to Him who is able to do immeasurably more than all we ask or imagine, according to His power that is at work within us, to Him be the glory in the church and in Christ Jesus throughout all generations forever and ever! Amen."

Since we are studying prayer, I will put the emphasis on Ephesians 6:10-20 --- putting on the full armor of God.

Football players and soldiers (for example) must have ALL their equipment in order to function properly in their sport or job. The same holds true for the Christian--- we too need our full armor to stand against the acts of the enemy. We need to put on the full armor of God.

PRAYER TO PUT ON THE WHOLE ARMOR OF GOD

Heavenly Father, I put on the armor of God with gratitude and praise. Father, You have provided all I need to stand in victory against the enemy and his kingdom.

➢ I take the belt of truth. I know the enemy cannot stand against the truth.

➢ I take the breastplate of righteousness. I declare I am by faith in right standing with God. The enemy must retreat before God's righteousness.

➢ I shod my feet with the gospel of peace. I thank God for His peace, which covers me through prayer.

➢ Above all, I take up the shield of faith, which will enable me to quench the fiery darts of the wicked one.

➢ I put on the helmet of salvation to protect my mind from the enemy's ways.

➢ I lift the sword of the Spirit--the written word of God, which will cut to pieces the snares of the enemy.

Praying always with all prayer and supplication in the Spirit, and watching thereunto with all perseverance and supplications for all the saints.

Taken from the commentary in the Dake Bible.

We need to put on the armor to equip ourselves to do battle against the enemy, who is always trying to destroy us. Ephesians 6:18 tells us praying in the Spirit (in tongues) is a mighty weapon. Evil is in this world, brought here by the enemy of our soul. We must stand strong as God says we are indeed conquerors!

We thank you, Father, for giving us all the tools we need to be victorious in Jesus! The blood of the sacred Lamb covers us. Hallelujah

INTERCESSION

INTERCESSORY PRAYER

Is it on your heart to become an intercessor? Do you hear the summoning of the Holy Spirit, calling you to prayer? The definition of an intercessor is: one who prays for another individual, standing in the gap for that person, one who prays for our or any other country, one who prays for peace, justice, God's grace in the love of His people --- it encompasses a host of holy assignments! Webster defines it as: "1. The act of interceding. 2. Prayer, petition or entreaty in favor of another." Every true Christian is actually an intercessor, and this is a God given desire. To intercede for another is to take their burden on in your prayer, asking God to intervene in their circumstances. It is the very heart of the Christian, and a very profound duty to be taken very seriously. The Holy Spirit will, many times, put someone or something on your heart to pray for. You will feel the "push" and when you do, pray right then and there! Do not put it off until a more convenient time. When you are called to pray, pray or you could forget and miss the opportunity God tried to entrust you with. Pray for yourself, that you DO NOT miss such opportunity! As we sow, so shall we reap. We need to consistently pray for our family (both biological and church), friends, associates --- the field is ripe with many needs. And most importantly, there are those we don't particularly "like," yet we have an obligation to pray for them too, especially if they are in danger of going to hell. Remember, GOD is the only true judge--- we don't need to help Him!

Job 42:10, "And the Lord turned the captivity of Job, when he prayed for his friends; also the Lord gave Job twice as much as he had before." This means that God healed Job and restored two fold all that he had before. Job's three friends needed him to pray for them. Job realized they were in worse shape than he was. Because Job was faithful to pray for his friends, God blessed him.

Hebrews 7:25 (NIV), "Therefore He is able to save completely, those who come to God through Him (Jesus), because He always lives to intercede for them.(us)" Jesus is our intercessor--- how awesome is that? As our high priest, Jesus is our advocate, the mediator between us and God. He looks after our interests and intercedes for us with God. Christ makes perpetual intercession before God for us and His continuous presence in heaven with the Father assures us that our sins have been paid for and forgiven. (Romans 8:33; Hebrews 2:17-18; 4:15-16; 9:24)

PRAYER FOR OTHERS

"Heavenly Father, I bring before You and the Lord Jesus one who is very dear to You and to me _____. I have come to see that Satan is blinding and binding him/her in awful bondage. This person is in such a condition that he/she cannot or will not come to You for help on their own. I stand in for him/her in intercessory prayer before Your throne. I draw upon the Person of the Holy Spirit that He may guide me to pray in wisdom, power and understanding.

In the name of the Lord Jesus Christ, I loose_____ from the awful bondage the powers of darkness are putting upon him/her. I bind all powers of darkness set on destroying his/her life. I bind them aside in the name of the Lord Jesus Christ and forbid them to work. I bind up all powers of depression that are seeking to cut _____.

Off and imprison him/her in a tomb of despondency. I bring in prayer the focus of the Person and work of the Lord Jesus Christ directly upon _____ to his strengthening and help. I bring the mighty power of my Lord's incarnation, crucifixion, resurrection, ascension and glorification directly against all forces of darkness seeking to destroy _____.

I pray, Heavenly Father, that You may open _____ eyes of understanding. Remove all blindness and spiritual deafness from his/her heart. As a priest of God in _____'s life, I plead Your mercy over his/her sins of failure and rebellion. I claim all of his life united together in obedient love and service to the Lord Jesus Christ. May the Spirit of the living God focus His mighty work upon

_____ to grant him/her repentance and to set him/her completely free from all that binds him/her.

In the name of the Lord Jesus Christ, I thank you for Your answer. Grant me the grace to be persistent and faithful in my intercessions for _____, that You may be glorified through this deliverance. AMEN."

Chaplain Tom Conti

WHAT SATAN FEARS MOST

What Satan fears most
Is a man on his knees
Not vast marching armies
With great weaponry.

He knows he can stand
Against the power of men
To engage us in battle
Is mere sport to him.

But a man on his knees
With his head bowed in prayer
Is something quite different
To the prince of the air.

For when he sees us in prayer
To our God most high
He knows we have seen
Through devilish lies.

That's why satan fears most
A man on his knees
And we will keep him trembling
If our prayers never cease.

TITHING FINANCIAL BLESSING

Financial blessing is something we all want. It is critical to understand the relationship between giving and receiving. Many churches are seeing less intake in their collections. If the principal of tithing was understood, there would never be a problem in our giving. For many, money is tight and we are tempted to give less than what we know we should. What is difficult to comprehend, however, is you cannot out give God--- if you tithe as you should, He will bless you.

Tithing honors the scriptural principles of generously providing for religious leaders, giving to those in need and laying up treasures in heaven. Proverbs 3:9-10, "Honor the Lord with thy substance and with the first fruits of all thine increase so shall thy barns be filled with plenty and thy presses shall burst out with new wine." Luke 6:38 (For those who have the red lettering in your bible, the following verse is in red indicating this was Jesus speaking) "*Give and it will be given to you. A good measure, pressed down, shaken together and running over, will be poured into your lap. For with the measure you use, it will be measured to you.*" Malachi 3:10, "Bring the whole thing into the storehouse, that there may be food in my house. "**Test me in this**" says the Lord Almighty (the only place in the bible where God says to test Him) and see if I will not throw open the floodgates of heaven and pour out so much blessing that you will not have enough room for it."

The storehouse was a place in the temple for storing grain and other food given as tithes. The priests lived off these gifts.

Many Christians struggle with the issue of tithing. In some churches, giving is over-emphasized. However, many Christians refuse to submit to the biblical exhortations about making offerings to the Lord. Tithing/giving is intended to be a joy and a blessing, but sadly, that is not always the case in today's church.

Not too long ago, I was Associate Pastor in a new, small church, which was just starting up, named Damascus Road. It only lasted about 6 months. The Senior Pastor did not like asking for money. He apparently was uncomfortable with that. Since I was the "Prayer Pastor", it was my duty to pray over the offerings. I used all the pertinent scriptures and the church was doing rather well. However, because of many reasons, the church did not flourish and shut down. When is dissolved, I prayed the parishioners had at least picked up on the scriptural relationship of giving and receiving, as this was so important to their spiritual growth.

As new Christians, we tithed on the net income, but due to better understanding, graduated to tithing on the gross. At that time, Janet and I had joined another church that was very small and struggling and it was the end of their fiscal year. I was on commission at my secular job, and Janet was an Executive Assistant at a large nursing home making a good salary but still we had difficulty balancing our budget and tithing was not our "normal" (spiritual) agenda yet. I already was aware, at years' end I would receive a larger than usual check. Knowing the amount needed to pay our bills, I made a "deal" with God---I would give all left over, after paying our bills, to the church even after paying our tithe. When I got paid, I was upset as it turned out to be much more than I had anticipated. I now fought with myself, trying to rationalize why I should NOT give that much away. But the Holy Spirit spoke to my heart and I did as I had promised. Our Pastor announced in service the church was not doing very well, financially, leaving the church in debt. At that service, I was not really paying much attention to what Pastor was saying, but God sure was! Later that day, I received a phone call from Pastor, thanking me for such a generous donation and informing me it was the exact amount, to the penny, of what they needed to cancel the debt! God is good, amen? He gave ME the blessing to bless that little church! **YOU CANNOT OUT GIVE GOD!** Proverbs 3:9-10 *"Honor the Lord with your wealth and the first fruits of all your crops; then your* *barns will be filled to overflowing and your vats will brim over with new wine."*

Since we began tithing, as we should, we have received financial blessing, it never ceases to amaze us. I was able to retire at 57 as God was in total control of my retirement plan! My wife also has been able to retire at 62 and we are so blessed to be able to be in full time ministry. We do many diverse facets of ministry, and we thank God for our many opportunities to serve Him! Hallelujah!

So, the best way to tithe correctly is when you get paid, write a check for 10% of your gross earning (before taxes) to the church you are part of. Offerings and missions are extra. If you ask God, He will tell you what to give. Be sure to pray with your spouse, as you are equally involved. Believe me when I tell you, you will be amazed at what God will do with your obedience! He WILL bless you abundantly! Remember too, always to be a good steward with the rest of your income.

I pray you will trust God in directing all your choices and decisions. When you are in line with His will, you are in line to receive His blessings!

WOULD YOU STEAL FROM GOD?

Whenever we hear about a church break-in, someone stealing from the house of God, we become enraged. However, we may be stealing from God without being aware of it!

The Old Testament suggests a 10% tithe. In the New Testament, it explains that it is all God's; we just need to keep what we need.

The following is from Bible.Org: Biblical Financial Stewardship:

"The most persuasive financial advice we get is the voice in our own head. Somewhere in the process of growing up we develop our own private financial philosophy. Our personal values are shaped by parents perhaps, but also learned by experience. Our financial mistakes made life unpleasant or maybe we experienced financial windfalls or had doting benefactors. But each experience marked our thinking. Altogether, that brought us to what we now believe and value about money and material possessions. Unfortunately, there is a universal flaw usually lurking in our well-tuned and often defended ideas. The flaw is that our ideas about money usually boil down to "what I think is best for me." Selfishness hides in every financial decision we make. Giving either makes me feel good or look good or a combination of both plus a tax benefit.

Could it be that our view of money is all about me? If there is another way to live, it will mean another way to think.

How God Thinks About Money:

Before Larry Burkett became a leading voice in the Christian world on the subject of money and material things, he was Christian businessperson who happened to lead a Bible study. One night he stated at the study that he had found over 100 verses in the bible about money. Someone responded by arguing that God was not that interested in the subject of our money. So Larry dug into the Bible and came back with over 700 verses highlighted about money in the Bible and started to organize them. Crown Financial

Ministries now says that there are actually about 2350 verses on finances and possessions in the Bible. That is more verses--more material--than all 13 letters in the New Testament that Paul wrote! God obviously cares about our view of possessions to instruct us that much about it.

Jesus said, "Where your treasure is, there will your heart be also." Matt 6:21 He is saying what we do with our money reveals our real priorities---it's that simple."

PRAY FOR YOUR ENEMIES

Romans 12:19 (NIV), "Do not take revenge, my friends, but leave room for God's wrath, for it is written, "It is Mine to avenge; I will repay, says the Lord."

Verse 20, "If your enemy is hungry, feed him; if he is thirsty, give him something to drink. In doing this, you will heap burning coals on his head."

Verse 21, Do not be overcome by evil, but overcome evil with good."

These verses are stating that by overcoming evil with good, you have already defeated the enemy's plan and God will take care of the judgment. That is never our part, as we never know the full story--- never know the heart of anyone, especially our enemies, so we are unable to judge as only God can.

Until we fully understand this concept, it is difficult to pray for someone with whom you are angry. The same goes for people who hurt you or those you fear. It goes against the initial response we humans tend to have in situations that are unpleasant or painful, and we want to strike back. That is not the Christian solution to any problem. We must keep in mind when someone hurts us in any capacity; our first response needs to be to pray for them to receive revelation of their wrongful behavior. Develop this attitude through the Holy Spirit, and by practicing, it becomes more natural and automatic. It's a discipline that takes time to achieve, but you will be successful through God's strength, not your own. Prayer develops so many parts of who we are and who we need to be as a believer. It reshapes our former experience, teaching and attitudes as we grow from glory to glory. You might say it gives us spiritual muscle and allows us to rise above petty former arguments. Prayer defeats the enemy's plan to form wrong information and responses. It allows us to recognize the lies and know who we are in Christ, giving us unshakable faith.

Matt 5:44, "But I say to you, love your enemies, bless them that curse you, do good to them that hate you, and pray for them that despitefully use you and persecute you." This is why forgiveness is so very important. God commanded we forgive, and as difficult as that may seem at times, we must forgive our enemies---period.

It is human to dislike our enemies, but it is divine to pray for them. The fact that Jesus commanded us to pray for our enemies distinguishes Christians from all others. Jesus did that on the cross. Luke 23:34 "Father forgive them for they know not what they do."

Father, I ask You to bless all my enemies (list them) and help me not to judge others as I shall be judged. Help me not to repay evil with evil. In Jesus's name, I pray.

PRAYER FOR SLEEP

Many people ask for prayer for a good night's sleep. When we are not physically tired, or if we have anxiety such as a pending big event, our minds focus on whatever is causing the anxiety and we cannot fall asleep. Rather than thinking about this, try praying! Prayer always gives you a comforting effect, knowing that the Lord is near and can help you through anything.

In the Old Testament days, they used Psalm 31:5, "Into Your hands I commit my spirit."

This worked for them, as did Psalm 91:11, "For You, God, will give Your angels charge over me to keep me in all my ways." You can insert you name when using this psalm.

God's angels do indeed protect the believer. They are present. That is truly a very calming thought.

If you still cannot sleep, ask God why! Possibly, there is someone God wants you to pray for. There may have been a divine appointment you missed today. It is not too late to pray. Review your day, thank God for getting you through it, and thank Him for tomorrow.

It may sound like an old cliché, but it's always good to count your blessings! You will find you come up with things you didn't recognize as a blessing before. Believers have so much to be thankful for! When you are Born Again, you have blessed assurance of your final destination and confirmation that you are sealed in the Holy Spirit. "In Him, you also, when you heard the word of truth, the good news of your salvation, and (as a result) believed in Him, were stamped with the seal of the promised Holy Spirit (the One promised by Christ) as owned and protected (by God.)" AMP version. As you go through all the blessings in your life, you will slowly drift off to sleep --- try it!

I cannot think of a better way to start and end your day than by reading the bible. Remaining close to God by knowing His Word will give you a sense of peace--the kind of peace only God can give. Stress melts away in His presence---- in the presence of Jehovah! Learn to trust His promises—they are all Yes and Amen! The relationship you form with the Father will give you the ability to relax and fall asleep peacefully at the end of your day.

I pray for you to get the sleep you need each and every night.

PRAYER FOR FREEDOM
FROM ANXIETY

Philippians 4:5-7 NIV

"Let your gentleness be evident to all. The Lord is near. Do not be anxious about anything, but in everything, by prayer and petition, with thanksgiving, present your requests to God. And the peace of God, which transcends all understanding, will guard your hearts and your minds in Christ Jesus."

What a beautiful, comforting promise! We need not worry or be anxious for ANYTHING when we fully believe and *know* God's Word! Matthew 6:25-34 goes into detail telling us not to worry about anything --- just seek and trust in God!

For those of you who seem to constantly be in a state of flux--frazzled and harried unable to gather your thoughts or be productive because you're always worried about something--usually what has not even happened yet, I suggest you memorize the above scriptures. Keep them in your heart so when you begin to feel anxious, just repeat these promises over and over until you experience God's comfort and peace. Tell Jesus how upset or worried you are and ask Him to help you find the peace He promised all believers. Take deep breaths and know He is near and He will help you.

The following are cures, according to scripture, for worry:

1. Permit the peace of God to keep your heart and mind guarded through Jesus Christ. Phil 4:7

2. Renounce all worry and by prayer, petition and thanksgiving make all requests known to God. Phil 4:6

3. Think on right (Godly) things. Phil 4:8

4. Keep your mind on God (He will keep you in perfect peace). Isaiah 26:3

5. Use the weapons of spiritual warfare. 2 Cor 10:4-5, "*The weapons we fight are not the weapons of the world. On the contrary, they have divine power to demolish strongholds. We demolish arguments and every pretension that sets itself up against the knowledge of God, and we take captive every thought to make it obedient to Christ.*" The definition of a stronghold is: A satanically energized argument designed to destroy us or block God's kingdom purposes in our lives.

6. Put on the whole armor of God. Eph 6:10-18

7. Have faith in God. Mark 11:22-24

8. Live and walk in the Spirit. Galatians 5:16

9. Do not cast away confidence. Hebrews 3:6 and 12--14.

10. Cast all care upon the Lord. 1 Peter 5:7, "*Cast all your anxiety on Him because He cares for you.*"

POWER

Dunamis means power in Greek. The Greek word is used 120 times in the New Testament. Loosely, the word refers to strength, power or ability and is the root word of our English words dynamic, dynamite, and dynamo.

Acts 1:8, *"But you shall receive power after the Holy Spirit has come upon you and you shall be witnesses unto Me both in Jerusalem and in all Judea and Samaria and unto the uttermost parts of the earth."*

2 Peter 1:3, *"His divine power has given us everything we need for life and godliness through our knowledge of Him who called us by His own glory and goodness."*

This divine power given to us by God is the object of the Christian calling. It enables us to live a life we could not live by our own strength. It is an empowering of our will to follow Jesus and live according to what the Bible teaches. We could never live the Christian life without such infilling of the Holy Spirit, who, from the moment we become Born Again seals us in Him.

Luke 24:49, *"I am going to send you what My Father has promised; but stay in the city until you have been clothed with power from on high."*

The promise is from Acts 2:1--4:

"When the day of Pentecost came, they were all together in one place. (The Upper Room) *Suddenly a sound like the blowing of a violent wind came from heaven and filled the whole house where they were sitting. They saw what seemed to be tongues of fire that separated and came to rest on each of them. All of them were filled with the Holy Spirit and began to speak in tongues as the Spirit enabled them."*

149

This is the spiritual baptism promised to all believers. This is the enabling to do the works of Christ. Once we receive the baptism of the Holy Spirit, we increase the effectiveness of our prayers. James 5:16 *"The prayer of a righteous man is powerful and effective."*

We need the Holy Spirit to help us pray. We know the revealed needs of ourselves and others, but the Holy Spirit knows the hidden needs. This is where tongues can be very beneficial as the Holy Spirit can pray *through* us even if we are unaware of the prayer being said. When the Spirit prays, the supernatural comes into operation and the miracles happen. Romans 8:26 *"In the same way, the Spirit helps us in our weakness. We do not know what we ought to pray for, but the Spirit Himself intercedes for us with groans that words cannot express."*

When you experience results from your prayers, your faith will increase and your holy confidence will strengthen you. You will come to the blessed knowledge that God is with you and He hears you---always. You may not always get the result you're looking for or expecting, but God is ever faithful to answer you--always! When you see the power at work because of your prayer, you will know God is using you to do His bidding.

Prayer is always such a wonderful conversation with the Lord. You can feel the flow of energy and the very presence of the God of the universe--- the Almighty everlasting God.

He who knows "every hair on your head" and created you for a time such as you're in, who loves you and wants to bless you, is *listening*. Cherish your time with Him and pray without ceasing! It moves mountains…prayer changes everything---it moves the hand of God.

Think back to situations that God has divinely intervened in your life. You may not have even recognized His intervention--given the credit to other sources. We need to be more aware of His presence and to be eternally grateful for His will for our lives.

Once you receive the baptism of the Holy Spirit, you will wonder how you ever functioned without it! You will move to the next level, spiritually, and depend on the holy power. Phil 4:13, *"I can do all things through Christ who strengthens me."*

The Lord wants us to have His gifts. He loves us so much He gave His only son to die for us. (John 3:16). We are special: Eph 2:10: *"For we are God's workmanship created in Christ Jesus to do good works which God has prepared in advance for us to do."*

What an honor it is to be a Christian!

Do not be afraid to accept the power and the gifts.

1 Corinthians 12:8-10 lists some of the Spiritual Gifts of God:

1. Word of wisdom
2. Word of knowledge
3. Faith
4. Healing
5. Miracles
6. Prophecy
7. Discerning of spirits
8. Tongues
9. Interpretation of tongues

We don't all receive all these gifts. Be grateful for the ones you do receive and use the gift frequently for the benefit of others as well as yourself. This is what God expects you to do and why you did in fact receive the gift (s). 1 Cor 12:11, *"All of these are the work of one and the same Spirit, and He gives them to each one just as He determines."*

THE PRAYER OF A RIGHTEOUS MAN....

James 5:16, "*Confess your faults one to another and pray for one another, that you may be healed. The effectual, fervent prayer of a righteous man avails much.*"

Back in the 1960's, there was a popular singing duo, The Righteous Brothers. They had many top selling records including "You Lost That Lovin' Feeling," "Unchained Melody," and "You're my Soul and Inspiration." It is interesting how they chose their name for the duo. One of the first times they sang together, at a local nightclub, a patron in the front row shouted out: "That's righteous, brother!" It fit-- the Righteous Brothers were born!

During a 2003 interview, Bill Medley, the surviving one of the duo was asked: "Being called the Righteous Brothers, did faith in God influence your career at all? His response: Yes, I give God all the credit because I know I am not smart enough to put this life of mine together without Him. Every time something wonderful happens, I just close my eyes and thank God for doing this for me. I thank Him for giving me the talent and the opportunity to share it."

Bill Medley is without a doubt one of the most significant voices in popular music history. He also has a humility and reverence for God, who indeed directs our paths.

(Excerpt taken from interview by Josh Belcher.)

Webster defines righteous as doing or according with what is right, just, upright, equitable, free from guilt or sin, Godly, holy, virtuous. Are you righteous with God?

The book of James tells us we need to be in right standing with God for our prayers to get great results. The Christian's most powerful resource is communion with God through prayer. The results are often greater than we thought possible. Some people see prayer as a last resort to be tried when all else fails. This approach is backward. Prayer should come first. Because God's power is infinitely greater than ours, it only makes sense to rely on it--especially because God encourages us to do so.

People sometimes fear they are not worthy, so they refrain from praying. They fear they are not right with God to be able to pray. If you just ask and trust God, He will tell you how to get right with Him ---- through His Word, through Christian leaders even through other Christians who are more advanced in their journey, but God is always listening. No one ever has to be "afraid" to pray, no matter what condition your heart and ways may be in. He is your source--- and He loves you and loves to hear you speak to Him through prayer. It doesn't have to be some formula or some prewritten prayer of any kind, it just needs to be your pouring out your heart and *trusting* your Holy Father. Never, never be afraid to go to God.

The word fervent means: hot, glowing, burning, zealous, passionate, intense. Fervent praying is praying as if your life, or the lives of those you are praying for depends on your prayers. Like a small child that has no reason to believe his prayers will not be answered. It praying with a passion and sense of urgency in complete trust that God is listening. It is an assurance that God can handle anything and that you can't! We think of Jesus in the Garden of Gethsemane, at the foot of the Mount of Olives in Jerusalem. He prayed so hard, droplets of blood appeared on His brow. Luke 22:44 " And being in anguish, He prayed more earnestly, and His sweat was like droplets of blood falling to the ground."

I am sure God does not expect us to pray as Jesus did that day, but we do need to be earnest in our partitions and thankful. We need to have no doubt that God will listen.

Not every prayer will be answered as we want or expect, but God will ALWAYS listen.

As you mature in your Christian walk and prayer life, you will understand so much more of what you need to know. Reading your bible everyday will certainly help you grow and the more you grow, the more you will realize how very important your prayers are.

My prayer is for anyone who is reading this book, may God bless you and give you the opportunity to develop a fervent prayer life!

JOB
THE POWER OF INTERCESSORY PRAYER

Job 42:10, "After Job had prayed for his friends, the Lord made him prosperous again and gave him twice as much as he had before."

Most of us are familiar with the book of Job. Job is named as one of the most patient and Godly men of the Bible. *Job 1:1, "In the land of Uz there lived a man whose name was Job. This man was blameless and upright; he feared God and shunned evil."*

According to the dateline of the Old Testament, Job is one of the oldest books of the Bible, possibly the very oldest, and it is a masterpiece. The actual author is unknown.

There are theories, but no one knows.

As written in the NIV Life Application Study Bible, "Job, the book, tells the story of Job, the man of God. It is a gripping drama of riches-to-rags-to-riches, a theological treatise about suffering and divine sovereignty, and a picture of faith that endures. As you read Job, analyze your life and check your spiritual foundation. May you be able to say that when all is gone but God, He is enough."

Job trusted God even when he did not understand why he was facing so many trials. We, too, must trust God when we do not understand the difficulties we face.

Job is an early example of intercessory prayer. When he *prayed for his friends* is the key. Job understood how unbalanced his friends were and that they needed his prayers. He felt that God was not happy with them.

We all can profit from this lesson. How many times have we missed the opportunity to pray for those around us? Ask the Holy Spirit to give you the ability to recognize when you should pray for someone. Many times, it should be right then and there---not to wait for a more comfortable time when you're alone. Even if you feel that you should not approach the person, you can still silently pray for them.

"What peace we often forfeit, oh what needless pain we bare, all because we do not carry everything to God in prayer." Joseph Scrivener "What a Friend We Have in Jesus," an 1855 hymn.

We often do not realize what a great privilege we have to be able to pray to our Father in Jesus' name. Jesus is our intercessor! *Romans 8:34, "Who is He that condemns? It is Christ that died, yea rather, that is risen again, who is even at the right hand of God, who also makes intercession for us."* What an amazing and comforting scripture that tells us our Lord, Jesus, intercedes for US! There are so many scriptures that make you feel so loved and so safe. This is another good reason to read your Bible daily. Drink from that fountain and grow in your faith.

When was the last time you prayed for your friends? How about for your enemies? Pray, especially, for those who do not know Jesus as Lord and Savior. Remember, it is not only for their benefit, but for yours. God will bless you for your compassion. God does not want anyone to perish. *2 Peter 3:9, "The Lord is not slow in keeping His promises as some understand slowness. He is patient with you, <u>not wanting anyone to perish</u>, but everyone to come to repentance."* It is an honor to pray for others as well as a duty for the believer. What God gives you, He expects you to pass on. He's given believers hope and we must give this to others.

Intercessory prayer is powerful. It is standing in the gap for others who are not yet enlightened and for those who need prayer for many other reasons. For those who are not walking with Jesus, especially family members, you can pray Ezek 36:26, *"Take his heart of stone and give him a heart of flesh."* Intercessory prayer can break chains of bondage, and peal the scales of unbelief.

We, as believers, all have a lot of work to do. Start today and *pray* for all God has put on your heart.

Chaplain Tom Conti

My prayer is that you will expand your prayer life, understand what a privilege prayer is and be sensitive to people around you.

GOD SPEAKS TO US/GOD DOES NOT SPEAK TO US

Over the years, this subject has been asked of me many times. Long-time, mature Christians have asked why God does not speak to them. The fact is, God does speak to them, but they are unable to recognize that it is God, or they may be unwilling to accept what He is telling them in their spirit. When we pray, we are talking to God. When we read the Bible, He is talking to us. God always answers prayer. It may not be what you are expecting or want, it may take a lot longer than you wanted, the answer may be a simple "no" which you do not want to accept, or it will be clear through circumstances, but there is always an answer.

Some time ago, there was a debate at our church between a Muslim cleric and a born again former Muslim cleric, who is now a Christian pastor. Present were about 250 Muslims and over a thousand Christians. The born again Pastor asked a question of the Christians: "How many of you have heard God speak to you?" About every Christian hand went up. He then asked the Muslims, "How many of you have heard Allah speak to you?" Of the 250 present, one hand was raised. Would you serve a God who speaks to you, or one who does not?

It is so vital for Christians to pray and read their Bible daily. We need to stay in touch; stay connected to our heavenly Father. It is part of our "daily bread" (our spiritual nourishment). It is the foundation of who we are as Christians and our lifeblood! The most important part of your day is the time spent with the Lord. This is when you can truly hear, in your spirit, the Almighty God speaking to *you*. How awesome is that? Learn to recognize that still, quiet voice and be thankful that you do. I cannot emphasize this discipline enough---prayer and Bible study are not just for Sundays. It should be the first thing you do every day. It doesn't have to be lengthy all the time, short prayers and some Bible study are valid too when necessary. God waits to hear from us. He wants to bless our day and us. It strengthens you to face what your day has in store, knowing God is with you!

Discernment is covered as a separate topic. The question is, when you're hearing something in your spirit, is it God, is it the devil or is it you? If it is God, it will *always* be based on scripture. If it is of the devil, it will have twisted scripture or something you know that you know that you know is not from God. And if it is coming from your mind, it will be the easy way out of something difficult to face. Not demonic, but not exactly what God would have you do. You will make excuses for something you know you should not say or do, but try to reason that it's OK.

Prayer is a dialogue not a monologue. I will be the first to say, it can be extremely difficult to remain still, keep your mind calm and listen for that still, quiet voice of the Lord through His Holy Spirit. It does take practice, patience and determination, but the rewards will be so worth the effort. In fact, the results are phenomenal! It is a whole higher dimension in your relationship with God, leaving you refreshed and strengthened.

When reading your Bible verses, go slowly so as to absorb the material. Bibles that have commentary are very helpful with understanding scripture. Be sure to read all of it. If you have a Bible with the red lettering, this signifies it is Jesus' actual words, so pay close attention. Scripture can be quoted, by you, later in the day or in the near future if the occasion arises. You will surprised at how much you do remember, as the Bible is life and the words are life and will be planted in your heart and spirit. Scripture is always such an encouragement to others as well as yourself. Everyone has their "favorite" verses or books and you will too, if you already don't. I find it difficult to imagine how people can get through life without knowing and praying the Word of God.

My wife and I have the esteemed honor to be altar counselors at our church. This is a God given appointment to us and we are so in awe to be chosen for this assignment. We pray beforehand for wisdom, guidance and the anointing to pray for our Lord's precious lambs. There is a transformation that goes through altar counselors, where our personalities step aside and the Holy Spirit takes over to flow through us as we pray for others. We truly consider this an awesome privilege.

One morning God gave me the scripture, Luke 17:5, *"The Apostles said to the Lord, increase our faith."* Although I am familiar with this scripture, I do not use it that often.

The next person that came to us for prayer asked to have his faith increased! God is so faithful to help us pray effectively. He will help you too---just ask Him. As it says in James 4:2 --- you have not because you ask not!

Perhaps you avoid listening for God's voice because you're afraid of what He may say. Perhaps you believe this would take you out of your comfort zone and make you uneasy.

God is always gentle and kind. He loves you and wants to bless you and hear from you. There is no reason to be afraid. None. He is your source of everything good.

If you are a born again believer, filled with the Holy Spirit, you should be hearing from God all the time. We are all at different places in our spiritual journey. God wants you to grow and your horizons to broaden. The closer to get to God, the better off you will be. Put all your faith, trust in Him now and forever, and listen for His counsel. It will definitely change your life.

THE JABEZ PRAYER

1 Chronicles 4:9, "Jabez was more honorable than his brothers. His mother had named him Jabez saying I gave birth to him in pain."

Jabez means sorrow or pain. Although all women endure pain in childbirth, Jabez's mother chose to name him because of her pain. This most likely was ridiculed by many of his friends as well as strangers.

1 Chronicles 4:10, "Jabez cried out to the God of Israel, 'Oh that you would bless me and enlarge my territory! Let your hand be with me, and keep me from harm so that I will be free from pain." And God granted his request."

The five requests were:

1. Bless me indeed
2. Enlarge my territory
3. Let Your hand be with me
4. Keep me from (evil) pain
5. Keep me from grief (suffering)

These are the most frequently heard from the average man. God heard Jabez and we have the same right to believe that He will hear us and all others who pray likewise from the heart. God is no respecter of persons. Romans 2:11 NIV, *"For God does not show favoritism."*

Bruce Wilkinson has written books on the Jabez Prayer. He suggests you repeat the prayer for 30 days and find out for yourself if your life changes. He believes it will.

As I have said in other parts of this book, you must pray according to God's Will. You cannot ask for something outlandish and expect your request to be granted! As you develop your walk with the Lord, you will understand, on a deeper level, what His will is for you and pray accordingly.

WALKING IN THE SPIRIT

Reflection on Prayer

1. *Oppression of the Spirit breaks fellowship from God.*

   Prov 12:25, 15:13, 17:22 and 18:14. James 5:13-14

2. *When we pray, we honor God by trusting Him.*

   Prov 3:5-10

3. *Sin or disobedience breaks fellowship with God. Satan "blocks in" our spirit.*

   Ps 66:18; Deu 28:23. 2 Kings 7:2 and 14.

4. *Draw close to God so He can hear you and you can hear Him.*

   James 4:7-8. Ps 28:12 and 69

5. *<u>Pray without ceasing!</u> Pray in the spirit and with understanding.*

   1 Thes 5:17

6. *Every prayer is presented to God—stored in heaven and answered in God's time.*

   Rev 5:8 and 8:3-4

Remember, the answer to your prayer many not be the answer you want, like or expected!

BLESSINGS AND CURSES

This is a difficult topic to address. Many strong Christians do not believe in curses, but have no problem believing in blessings. In this world, however, there are always opposites--plus and minus, black and white, good and evil.

Cursing in the Bible is not only speaking evil of someone, but evil coming upon someone. If a person is under a curse, according to the Bible, evil has come upon them in some way. This does not mean that every difficult circumstance we go through is a curse. Sometimes God leads us through a circumstance to stretch our faith.

Blessings are mentioned over 500 times in the Bible, curses a little over 200.

I have been going to church for a long time and I cannot recall this topic ever being addressed. It seems to be uncomfortable for pastors to talk about curses, although they never have a problem addressing blessings. Pastors rather preach how blessed we are, and that is good to know! Nevertheless, like it or not, address it or not, curses are also real.

Let us look at some scriptures:

Genesis 12:2-3, *"I will make you into a great nation and I will bless you; I will make your name great and you will be a blessing. I will bless those who bless you and whoever curses you, I will curse, and all the peoples on earth will be blessed through you.'*

This is God speaking to Abraham and is the only place in the Bible this is found. This is why today; we must bless the Jewish people, Israel.

Genesis 27: 29, *"May nations serve you and peoples bow down to you. Be lord over your brothers, and may the sons of your mother bow down to you. May those who curse you be cursed and those who bless you be blessed."*

This is Isaac's prayer over his son; Jacob who he thought was Esau. I suggest you read all of Genesis 27 to understand the story of Isaac and his two sons.

If you are thinking this is "only" Old Testament, let us look at New Testament scriptures:

Galatians 3:13, *"Christ redeemed us from the curse of the law by becoming a curse for us, for it is written: Cursed is everyone who is hung on a tree."*

Deuteronomy 21:23, *"You must not leave His body on the tree overnight. Be sure to bury Him that same day, because anyone who is hung on a tree is under God's curse."*

Galatians 3:14, *"He redeemed us that the blessings given to Abraham might come to the Gentiles through Christ Jesus, so that by faith we may receive the promise of the Spirit."*

Jesus Christ became a curse for us so we could receive the blessing of being saved. He bore our sins and died that we may live. Hallelujah!

Jesus is speaking in Matthew 5:44, *"But I say unto you, love your enemies, bless them that curse you, do good to them that hate you, and pray for them who despitefully use you, and persecute you."* This same theme is carried out in Luke 6:28 and Romans 12:14.

Your choice--- do you want to be blessed or cursed? Not a difficult decision I would say!

Here's a little test:

Take two small flowerpots and plant a seed in each. Say blessings over one. Water it and nurture it, then ignore the other saying curses over it. See what happens. See which one will grow!

SECRET THINGS

Deut. 29:29, "The secret things belong to the Lord our God, but the things revealed belong to us and to our children forever, that we may follow all the words of this law."

This is man's answer to every puzzling question concerning God and His plan.

"There are some secrets God has chosen not to reveal to us, possibly for the following reasons: (1) our finite minds cannot fully understand the infinite aspects of God's nature and the universe. (Ecclesiastes 3:11); (2) some things are unnecessary for us to know until we are more mature;(3) God is infinite and all knowing, and we do not have the capacity to know everything He does. This verse shows us that although God has not told us everything there is to know about obeying Him, He has told us enough. Thus disobedience comes from an act of the will, not a lack of knowledge. Through God's word we know enough about Him to be saved by faith and to serve Him. We must not use the limitation of our knowledge as an excuse to reject His claim on our life."

Excerpt taken from commentary in NIV Bible.

In the movie, "A FEW GOOD MEN," Jack Nicholson tells Tom Cruise in one intense courtroom scene "You cannot handle the truth….." God knows there are times we cannot either! Because our capacity to understand is limited, we must have faith in God, and trust Him to reveal whatever He wants us to know, as only He knows what we are able to handle. The enemy will always try to plant doubt in your heart. We must pray for God's protection and wisdom. Wisdom to recognize the enemy's voice and ways.

We need to thank God and give Him all the glory for sparing us--- for keeping the "secret things."

Never get discouraged and stop reading your bible and/or stop praying because you don't understand what is going on and why. Sometimes there are reasons beyond our comprehension, and we need to draw close to Jesus and not fear, because God always knows best and is always in control of everything in our life. Through all your pain and sorrow, He is there. You were never promised a life without pain, but you ARE promised God will see you through. Just trust Him. There are times you cannot reason and figure everything out. This may appear to be a very dark time, but *He is there.*

Try to dwell on all the positive things in your life. The times--- those glorious moments when our prayers are answered and we are victorious. The many times scripture comes alive for us and we can recognize God speaking to our spirit, the praise reports we got and the miracles we witnessed. You will discover they out number all the times you couldn't understand your circumstances.

Early on in our prayer ministry, my wife and I were in a situation. A friend of ours was having surgery to remove a portion of her brain. We were influenced by others praying for God to take her home, as according to her doctors, even if she survived the surgery, she would be in a vegetative state. So, we also prayed for God's mercy in taking her home. But God had other plans for her! She not only survived the surgery, she was her normal, functioning self!! This was a lesson learned for my wife and the others as well as I. Never again will we pray negative. The doctors can give their educated opinion, and do what they are well trained to do, but only God can heal. Only God can take what looks hopeless and turn everything (logical) around!

Mark 11:23-24, "I tell you the truth, if anyone says to this mountain, go throw yourself into the sea and does not doubt in his heart but believes that what he says will happen, it will be done for him. Therefore, I tell you, whatever you ask for in prayer, believe that you received it and it will be yours."

166

The kind of prayer that moves mountains is prayer for the fruitfulness of God's kingdom. It would seem impossible to move a mountain into the sea, so Jesus used that picture to say that God can do anything.

God will answer your prayers, but not because of your mental attitude. Other conditions must be met: (1) you must be a believer; (2) you must not hold a grudge against another person; (3) you must not pray with selfish motives; (4) your request must be for the good of God's kingdom. To pray effectively, you need faith in God, not faith in the object of your request.

When we pray, we can express our desires, but want His will above ours. Check yourself to see if your prayers focus on your interests or God's.

When we go home to glory, we will know the "secret things," as our spirit is perfect in Jesus and all will be revealed to us who love Him.

I pray you will constantly increase your faith, pray about everything and leave the secret things to the Lord.

FISHERS OF MEN

Luke 5:10, "... Then Jesus said to Simon, "Don't be afraid, from now on you will catch men."

This was Jesus speaking to James, John and Peter (called Simon) after the miraculous catch of fish.

We (believers) are all fishers of men. The most important prayers we all should be praying daily are for salvation for our loved ones. Pray for your family, friends, neighbors and anyone needing salvation. Pray even for those you know need it, but do not particularly like or care about them. You don't have to "love" someone in order to pray for them. God will put all sorts of personalities into your life that He wants you to pray for. In this case, your feelings do not count---only their salvation does!

2 Peter 3:9, "The Lord is not slow in keeping His promise, as some understand slowness. He is patient with you, not wanting anyone to perish, but everyone to come to repentance."

This explains why God has delayed so long in putting down all rebellion and in tolerating His enemies to continue their evil designs.

A pastor I knew prayed for his older brother for many years. The brother was then close to death due to cancer. This pastor told his brother that he would not let death take him until he received Jesus Christ as Lord and Savior. After holding out for a few more days, the brother finally conceded and accepted His Lord. He died very soon after. This is how we ought to treat our unsaved family. God's Holy Spirit is always there to turn around the most convicted non-believer and our prayers help in the process. Pray Ezekiel 36:26 for God to take their heart of stone and give them a heart of flesh.

When I was in Vietnam in 1967, I would attend the Sunday service if possible. About half the time, I was on a mission and unable to attend. Most of the time the Chaplin could not be there either. He would give the duty to his assistant, John. John approached me one Saturday evening carrying his large, red bible and telling me he was unable to do the service the next day. He then asked me to do it! I was overwhelmed! Before I could protest, he showed me the scripture he had marked in his bible. It was Luke 5:11--the story of the miracle catch and the prophecy that the Apostles would become fishers of men.

I had "made a deal" with God before I went to Vietnam: if He got me through it, I would serve Him. This was a seed starter for me. It took me until 1994 as there was a lot of watering to be done for me to truly become a fisher of men. Looking back at about twenty-two years of ministry, I thank God for being patient with me and for His calling on my life.

Romans 11:29, "for God's gifts and His call are irrevocable."

God very rarely will change His mind and He never makes mistakes. Men may fail Him so He is unable to fulfill such callings in them. But when, if ever, they come back to repentance, God will hold them to the original obligation to serve and obey Him.

If you are not praying for the salvation for all you know, now is a good time to start. Make a list and do not neglect continually to add to it. Our work is not done until we go home to glory.

I pray for Father God to give us the energy and desire to intercede for all unsaved You put in our path. Help us to be persistent for we know You wish none to perish.

A NEW MAN IN CHRIST

A PRAYING MAN

2 Corinthians 5:17, *"Therefore if any man be in Christ, he is a new creature; old things have passed away; behold, all things are become new."*

Someone once said, men do not ask directions, do not eat quiche and do not pray.

Are you a "new" man (or woman) in Christ? Born again Christians pray! When you were the old person, you had many bad habits, but now that you are a new creature, these old ways should have been cast out. Godly habits must replace the old rebellious ones. Prayer is a *good* habit! The Holy Spirit who now dwells in you will guide your choices and decisions. Perhaps you formerly did not pray very often--- perhaps not at all, but you probably had "good intentions," wanting good things for your loved ones and yourself.

Ephesians 4:22-24, *"You were taught, with regard to your former way of life, to put off your old self, which is being corrupted by its deceitful desires; to be made new in the attitude of your minds; and to put on the new self, created to be like God in true righteousness and holiness."*

The old man has been in the shackles of sin-- the chains binding (stopping) him to move forward in the Lord's way. But the new man is now covered by the precious blood of the sacred lamb. And he prays. Daily. Always. Both outward and inward sin must pass away. This was the way of your former self, the self that was dying. But now, in Christ, you are cleansed and forgiven! Hallelujah!

To become an effective prayer person, especially from the beginning, you do not need to quote scripture or have eloquent speech, pretending to be someone you're not. Just get alone with God and talk to Him.

170

Tell Him what is going on in your life and heart. Yes, He does already know, but this is for *your* comfort, and God wants to hear it from you. Be yourself, pray aloud and pour out your deepest concerns. He is your heavenly Father who created us for fellowship. Isn't it wonderful that we can always go to Him and find such peace? That's what following Christ and living the Christian life brings you. Never forget to approach Him with thanksgiving. Thank Him for your salvation and for all the many, many other blessings in your life!

1 John 1:7, *"But if we walk in the light, as He is in the light, we have fellowship with one another and the blood of Jesus Christ His son purifies us from all sin."*

2 Timothy 3:16-17, *"All scripture is God-breathed and is useful for teaching, rebuking, correcting and training in righteousness, so that the man of God may be thoroughly equipped for every good work."*

DON'T LOSE HEART

Luke 18:1, *"And he spoke a parable unto them to this end, that men ought always to pray and not to faint."* (Not lose heart.)

Not lose heart: do not give into doubt, fear, unbelief, and/or discouragement or use excuses for unbelief when prayers are not answered immediately. Rebuke and resist all opposition and all suggestions of failure. It is a divine, blood-bought right to get an answer. Just keep in mind it may not be the answer you wanted or expected, but God does answer prayer, and we must learn to trust Him that it is always the *right* answer.

Every Christmas season, I watch "It's a Wonderful Life," which came out in 1946, and remains an American classic. The movie is a fantasy/drama about George Bailey, played by James Stewart, a man who gave up his dream in order to help others. When George is in a desperate situation, heaven sends an angel to help. The angel questions, "Is George sick?" and God answers, "Worse, he is discouraged."

We have all been discouraged at one time or another. Life does have it's ups and downs, but we must not get discouraged, but trust in God that He has everything under control, even though at times, it doesn't appear that way. As Luke 18:1 says, do not lose heart.

Luke 18:2 is the parable of the unjust judge and the widow. *"He (Jesus) said: In a certain town there was a judge who neither feared God nor cared about men. And there was a widow in that town who kept coming to him with the plea, 'Grant me justice against my adversary.'* This widow was so persistent, she wore the judge down and he relented and gave the widow what she asked. She did not lose heart!

How many times a day do you stop and pray? You need not wait for something to go wrong, but thank God everything is alright! God is in all the "small stuff." Thank Him for a good parking spot, a lovely, sunny day, a green light, the smile on your baby's face, the soft fur and delight of your pet. It is endless what we have to be thankful for---we just need to recognize and understand that. Know how blessed you really are! God wants to be involved with everything in our lives. Perhaps your earthly father wasn't as attentive to you, but God always wants to be close and enjoys your fellowship and hears your prayers.

George Bailey was not much different than us. He tried to fix everything himself. He went to others, even his rival to beg for help. When all failed he did what he should have done first--- he prayed. He's a fictional character, but he depicts what we also do.

I have been there. Even after decades of prayer and teaching, I sometimes want to run to a mortal friend instead of the Father. What a comfort to know I can always rely on those everlasting arms!

LIBERTY IN PRAYER

Hebrews 3:6, *"But Christ is faithful as a son over God's house. And we are His house, if we hold onto our courage and hope of which we boast.*

Because Christ lives in us as believers, we can remain courageous and hopeful to the end. We are not saved by being steadfast and firm in our faith, but our courage and hope do reveal that our faith is real. Without this enduring faithfulness, we could easily be led astray by temptation, false teaching or persecution.

Believers have liberty of access to God. This is what prayer is. It is our right to go to the throne because Jesus died for us to give us this liberty.

Acts 4:13, *"When they saw the courage of Peter and John and realized they were unschooled, ordinary men, they were astonished and took note that these men had been with Jesus."* The people of this day realized that being with Jesus changed these men and gave them boldness in their prayer. They were able to have absolute confidence in access to God because all sins, which separated us from Him, were removed. In the Old Testament, men were not permitted to approach God. Even the mountain on which God gave the law was not to be touched by man. Only the high priest was permitted in the holy of holies once a year, and even then he could not approach God without proper atonement. Now, we have access to God by the blood of Jesus. (Hebrews 10:19-22.)

As long as we hold fast to this liberty of access to God, we are His house.

If there is unconfessed sin in our lives, or sin we hold on to, we do not have this liberty of access. God will not hear our prayers. Ps 66:18 *"If I had cherished sin in my heart, the Lord would not have listened."* and Isaiah 59:2 *"But your iniquities have separated you from your God."* We are *all* sinners saved by Grace, but be careful not to remain in a continuous cycle of committing the same sin over and over without any intention of stopping that sin. When you do sin, confess it to God and turn *away* from it.

You are missing God's blessings if you are not praying about everything all the time. We have the liberty (and the honor), and the freedom to go to the throne all the time. We need to practice using our liberty to do so. Start today and make it a habit!

My prayer for you: Father God, you know our hearts. We have no merit of our own on which to base any answer of prayer. We throw ourselves on your mercy because without you, we are nothing. In Jesus's name with thanksgiving, we pray.

HOW LONG SHOULD YOU PRAY?

1 Thessalonians 5:17: "Pray Without Ceasing"

How long should you pray? There is no appropriate amount of time. You need to ask the Holy Spirit and He will guide you. Usually, you will sense a fullness of spirit whereby you will know you have prayed enough for that particular time. Everyone has different agendas, priorities, needs and reasons to pray for others, and we are all on a separate journey with the Lord. Depending on where you are in your spiritual walk, start small, end big. As you grow, you will discover your prayers will too. The Holy Spirit will bring many things you weren't even aware of to light and you will know you need to pray for what is put on your heart. Prayer is such a beautiful privilege, given to us by the Almighty God so that we can talk to Him and commune with Him. It is such a comfort and the more we pray, the closer we will feel to our Father, and the closer we get, the more He will reveal to us. Awesome!

If you are a new believer, to pray without ceasing may seem like an unattainable goal! You may feel overwhelmed at the very thought of it, and it may even be discouraging causing you to feel unable to pray at all! This is exactly what the enemy of our soul wants. Do not be intimidated by thinking you could never pray like that. Just pray as much and as often as you feel you want to. As you advance in your journey, you will discover you are praying more and more--it becomes like a second nature to you. There are no specific formulas designed to instruct you how and when to pray. No special setting or time of day or whether you should be on your knees or flat on the floor. Don't trouble yourself with any of that --- just be content knowing you can pray whenever you feel the desire. You will be delighted how this will increase in time.

In time, God will give you "divine appointments" putting people in your path that He wants you to pray for. You will learn, through the Holy Spirit, how to recognize these times and through these appointments,

God will increase your prayer life. When you feel in your heart, God has placed someone before you for prayer, do not wait or hesitate. Ask the person if it is all right for you to pray for them and then do so. If they are not comfortable with prayer at that moment, that's OK---- pray for them silently, or when you walk away from them. God hears those prayers as well. You may dream about someone who needs prayer, or God will just put someone on your heart you haven't thought about for a long time, or even someone you know well. Just take a moment and pray for them.

"Smith Wigglesworth was an extraordinary student in the school of faith. A man wholly yielded to the Spirit, Wigglesworth became a "Pentecostal phenomenon," a vessel of God's supernatural power. This legendary preacher cast out demons, healed the sick, and stirred up passion for God in the hearts of thousands." (Taken from cover of book, "*The Anointing of His Spirit.*") Wigglesworth was known as a man of prayer and deep faith. When asked by an interviewer how long he prayed, he quickly answered five minutes.

This was not the answer this interviewer expected! How could such a powerful man of God only pray for five minutes? When asked for an explanation, Smith Wigglesworth replied with a smile, "Yes, I pray for five minutes, then go about my business for five minutes, then stop and pray again for five minutes." During the course of the day, this was a lot of prayer!

Prayer is not an option. It is a necessity!

"A PERSON OF PRAYER:

➢ Knows that prayer is a sacred trust from God.

➢ Understands his or her purpose in life as God's priest and intercessor for the world.

➢ Has a relationship of trust with the heavenly Father and desires the world to experience the power of His presence and life.

➢ Knows that the will of God will flow forth from heaven to earth only through his prayers and the prayers of all God's people.

God's will can be executed only through the cooperation of humankind on earth. Prayer is this medium of cooperation. Prayer is therefore the most important activity of humanity.

If we want to see God's will done on earth, we must do our part-- we must *pray.*"

(Excerpt from "Prayer" by Dr. Myles Munroe.)

My prayer is for you to become a person of prayer and thanksgiving.

EVERY TIME I HEAR A SIREN...

My wife and I have lived in Florida since January, 2002. We were only here a short time when I witnessed an accident involving an EMT wagon and a car. The EMT rig had flattened the car so badly that not only could you not tell the make and model of the car, you could not determine the color! At that very moment, God spoke to me to pray every time I heard a siren, and I do and always will.

I pray: *Father God, in Jesus name I pray, please send your holy angels to surround and deliver those emergency vehicles in a safe and swift manner. If when they arrive to help someone in danger---someone on the brink of death who does not know Jesus as Lord and Savior, please give them the opportunity to accept Jesus before they pass on to eternity.*

I have had the blessing to know a mighty man of God who is a missionary, and for a season, my mentor.

He had been to Russia a few times, and this one time he told the following story. He was in Moscow, teaching conferences each night for many nights. One evening he and his interpreter were walking in downtown Moscow when they came across an auto accident. A man was dead, lying on the road. The police were waiting for the body to be picked up. Compassion arose in this missionary's heart for this dead man. He heard, in his spirit, God telling him to pray for that man. The missionary was reluctant to do this because in Russia one must be very careful what they do. Many Russians were open to evangelism, but there were limits and boundaries of where and when to do what. But he knew he could trust God. Through the interpreter, he asked the police if he could pray for the dead man. They laughed, probably thinking what a crazy American, but finally they said OK.

The missionary knelt down and put his hand on the dead man's head. Everyone was watching and a silence filled the cold air. He first prayed for God's help in the way He wanted him to pray. In as clear a voice as this missionary has ever heard, God told him to pray, if this man did not know Jesus as Lord and Savior, may he live so he can be saved, so this is what he prayed and the man sat up! The crowd was in shock and awe! The man not only lived, he did accept Jesus and promised to attend the next meeting to give his testimony. I would guess, there were others in that crowd that was deeply inspired that night, and they too accepted Jesus. We serve such a mighty God, a God who still performs miracles!! Hallelujah! Although the missionary did not, that day, hear a siren yet, he was in a situation where he soon would as an ambulance had been summoned. It was he who also encouraged me to pray whenever I heard a siren.

God also had a plan for this missionary to be there at the very moment in time. When he was at the airport, getting ready to purchase his ticket to Russia, he realized he did not have enough money to buy the ticket. He immediately prayed for God to provide a way. Everything else was in order and set to go, he just needed to get to Russia. God told him to approach the ticket counter, which he did. When he told the attendant his name, before he could say anything else, the attendant handed him his ticket, which was in an envelope with his name on it. Someone had already purchased his ticket! Could this be anything but God? Praise the Lord for His provision and blessings! So, this missionary was able to be at that exact time and place to pray for the man who died and was brought back to life.

This missionary, a very ordinary, simple man, who loved, trusted and obeyed God, was able to bring an entire company of Russian soldiers to the Lord. Our God has no boundaries--nothing is impossible with Him and He will work through ordinary people to do extraordinary miracles.

The power of prayer is endless! Always be alert for divine appointments.

DELAYED PRAYER

I have used Daniel, Chapter 10, many times as an example of spiritual warfare. If you read that chapter, and I encourage you to do so, you will understand that it truly is. It also is an example of a prayer request being delayed.

The book of Daniel centers on this profound truth: the sovereignty of God.

Daniel was a prophet; one of God's highly esteemed. When he prayed, he received answers as he had a close relationship with the Lord. One day, however, when he prayed, he did not receive an answer, so he knew what he must do. He fasted for 21 days, eating no choice food and no meat or wine. During his fast, he was in continual prayer. He ate enough of food he didn't particularly like just so he would sustain himself. Some churches have the congregation do a "Daniel Fast" at various times. This is to commit to more intense times of prayer, and can be beneficial to both body and spirit.

God gave Daniel revelation and the understanding of the message came to him in a vision. In this vision, he saw a man dressed in linen with a belt of finest gold, who had a body like chrysolite, his face like lightening and eyes like flaming torches, his arms and legs like burnished bronze with a voice like the sound of a multitude. (Dan 10:4-6)

The man seen by Daniel was a heavenly being. Some commentators believe it was Christ, others think it was an angel because Michael's help was required. In either case, Daniel caught a glimpse of the battle between good and evil supernatural powers.

Daniel 10:12-13, "...Do not be afraid Daniel. Since the first day that you set your mind to gain understanding and to humble yourself before your God, your words were heard, and I have come in response to them. But the prince of the Persian kingdom resisted

me 21 days. Then Michael, one of the chief princes, came to help me, because I was detained there with the king of Persia."

So, although God sent a messenger to Daniel, a powerful spiritual being (prince of the Persian kingdom) detained the messenger for three weeks. Daniel faithfully continued praying and fasting, and God's messenger eventually arrived, assisted by Michael, the archangel. Unseen obstacles may hinder answers to our prayers. Don't expect God's answers to come too easily or quickly. Evil forces so pray fervently and pray earnestly may challenge prayer. Then expect God to answer at the right time.

We must keep in mind this powerful story, know that we must be persistent in our prayers, and not give up. Remember, the answer won't always come in the way and time you want and/or expect it, but keep praying --- God is *always* in control and His timing is always perfect!

FASTING

Webster's Dictionary defines fasting as: "To abstain from food, or to eat sparingly and only certain kinds of food, as by way of religious discipline."

It is actually an act of self-denial, and one can fast from other things besides food such as TV, your phone, radio, reading, sports--anything done on a regular basis for pleasure and enjoyment.

Let us first address the health benefits of fasting.

In Europe, they fast regularly on the changing seasons, as to prepare the body. When we fast, our energy level goes up as about 33% of our energy is used for digestion. Surely, you have experienced the desire to sleep after a large meal, such as what we consume around the holidays for example. After a time of fasting, the body will use what is available to burn stored up reserves in various organs etc. Most of us have junk stored in our liver and other areas. One who regularly fasts will have a cleaner system, seldom experience arthritis, usually have low body mass and they will look and feel great. Most will not have a weight problem. But the best part is---you will feel more closely connected to the Lord.

Bible Fasts:

There are 35 fasts mentioned in the Bible, from 1 day to 40 days and most are in the Old Testament. It is a biblical doctrine to fast, meaning no food for a length of time, but drinking plenty of water. The reason for fasting, besides being good for your health, is to spend this time in prayer. Fasting does not change God. He is the same before, during and after your fast, but it will change *you*. By keeping your flesh under holy discipline, it will help you become more sensitive to the Spirit of God. There are no set rules for this, about how long you should fast. It could be 24 hours or 3 days or longer. That should be between you and the Holy Spirit. The time you would normally be preparing and eating food, you would instead spend with the Lord and in prayer.

Prayer and Fasting:

These two disciplines go together. We need to fast and pray when under judgment, 1 Kings 21:27; in need, Ezra 8:21; in danger, Ester 4; worried Daniel 6:18; in trouble, Acts 27:33; in spiritual conflict, Matt 4:1-11 and when desperate in prayer Acts 9.

Fasting has worked miracles when used with prayer and faith! Many Pastors, Evangelists, intercessors etc. will fast before ministering. I teach at Teen Challenge on Tuesday mornings, so I fast from after dinner on Monday evening until dinner on Tuesday evening. My wife and I are altar councilors at our church on Sunday mornings, so we do not have anything to eat until after church. We want to be "prayed up" and alert without having any digestion going on!

PRAYER OR NO PRAYER?

Some time back, for a season, I was privileged to lead a weekly prayer service. We would gather to pray before the Wednesday evening service at church. It was a group of twenty or so consisting mostly of women. We would pray for the upcoming service, the Pastor, the music etc. and welcome the Holy Spirit in our midst. We would then have a time of prayer requests and praise reports.

One of the women had a request for her twenty-year-old grandson who had been arrested for drugs with the intent to distribute. He was looking at 10 years hard time. We all stood in agreement for favor with the judge. Some weeks later, she had a praise report! Her grandson had found abundant favor. By the mercy of the court and GOD, he had been given time served and probation. There could be no other explanation except that God had intervened and moved that judge to rule in the grandson's favor. Do you understand how prayer works? Do you see, by this testimony, that ALL things are possible with God? One of the other ladies in our group tearfully shared that *her* son did get 10 years for a similar charge. She was unaware of his situation until he had already been sentenced, so *no one had prayed for him.* Two young men, same type of crime, totally different results because one had been covered in prayer, the other wasn't.

If we only knew the power there is in prayer we would do a LOT more praying, amen? When we do pray, we need to pray like our lives and the lives of our loved ones depended on those prayers because ----they DO! Praying should be as easy and as natural as breathing. Just to realize that when in prayer, the Almighty God of the Universe is listening. He is THERE with you! We are so blessed to have this privilege to come before the Lord and present our requests, but we also have an obligation to pray for others. Not only our family and loved ones, but all those who desperately need Jesus. In any emergency, pray should be our first response. I cannot emphasize enough, how much power there is in prayer. It can move mountains and give you the deepest form of comfort and peace. It is our heavenly Father's means of communicating with His children, and it is for our benefit ALWAYS. Even when we pray for others, it is a blessing to us to be able to do so. I pray about *everything* and it has blessed me beyond what I can express!

May God bless you with an increased prayer life!

JOHN 3:16

"For God so loved the world, that He gave His only begotten Son, that whosoever believeth in Him should not perish but have everlasting life."

Just meditate on that scripture and drink in it's meaning. God sent His only son to die for us sinners so that we would have life everlasting if we accepted this gift! Our Father sent Jesus to die so we may live. Wow........

"The entire gospel comes to a focus in this verse. God's love is not static or self-centered; it reaches out and draws others in. Here God sets the pattern of true love, the basis of all love relationships---when you love someone dearly, you are willing to give freely to the point of self-sacrifice. God paid dearly with the life of His son, the highest price He could pay. Jesus accepted our punishment, paid the price for our sins and then offered us the new life that He had bought for us. When we share the gospel with others, our love must be like Jesus'--willing giving up our own comfort and security so that others may join us in receiving God's love." (commentary from NIV Bible.)

Back in 2013 as I was preparing to work on this book, I had the golf match on TV. It was the President's cup. I had decided to use John 3:16 along with three other scriptures concerning who can be saved. Moments before Tiger Woods clinched the win for the US Team, the camera focused on a fan holding a large sign with John 3:16 written on it. I loved seeing that! I had seen this scripture on display at football games, but this was a first at this golf match. Believers *know* the deep meaning of John 3:16, and it is always good that this is shared with those who do not, and we are privileged, in America, to still be allowed to voice our belief in God's truth!

Because of the profound truth of John 3:16, it is one of the most used scriptures in the bible. When Tim Tebow wrote this scripture on his face during his last game in Florida, about 350,000 people Googled it! God is certainly using Tim.

Sadly, there are people who are repulsed by the idea of eternal life because their lives are miserable. But eternal life is not an extension of a person's miserable, mortal life. Eternal life is God's life embodied in Christ given to all believers now as a guarantee that they will live forever. In eternal life there is no death, sickness, sorrow, tears, enemy, evil or sin. When we do not know Christ, we will make choices as though this life is all we have. In reality, this life is only the temporary existence where we must make our choice to believe and accept Jesus Christ as our Lord and Savior or reject Him. To believe is more than intellectual agreement that Jesus is God. It means to put our trust and confidence in Him that He alone can save us.

WHO CAN BE SAVED?

How should we pray for lost family members, friends and those who are lost? We need to stand on God's word and trust that our Father hears and will use our prayers for them. A beginning request would be quoting Ezekiel 36:26, *"I (God) will give you a new heart and put a new spirit in you. I will remove from you your heart of stone and give you a heart of flesh."* So, YOU are asking the Lord to remove their heart of stone and give them a heart of flesh, which means a heart that is no longer hardened.

No matter how impure anyone's life is right now, God offers a fresh start. Those you pray for can receive a new heart for God, and have His spirit within them. Prayer works. Be persistent and trust God to touch them in a way only HE can. You have no way of knowing what will result; you just need to rely on God.

For us Christians, it is very difficult to know someone we love is not saved----yet. We know how urgent it is for them to accept Jesus and we can be very impatient. But, we must just keep on praying and believing God will hear our prayers and honor them in *His* timing. WE can't save anyone or change anyone's mind---that is God's part. Our part is to trust God and keep praying.

My wife and I have been prayer warriors and altar counselors for many years and we have had so many requests for salvation. People that feel they cannot be saved for whatever reason and are carrying this heavy burden need to hear the good news! They need to understand how much God loves them and is ready and willing to accept them, and most of them are coming to the altar or to people they know are God's people, because someone, somewhere is praying or has prayed for them! The enemy is a liar! The enemy lies to people that they cannot be saved. As we grow in faith, we learn to recognize his lies and rebuke him, as he will lie to Christians too. This is why we must know God's word----so we know when we are being deceived.

1 Timothy 1-4, *"I urge then, first of all, that requests, prayers, intercession and thanksgiving be made for everyone--for kings and all those in authority, that we may live peaceful and quiet lives in all Godliness and holiness. This is good and pleases God our Savior, WHO WANTS ALL MEN TO BE SAVED AND COME TO THE KNOWLEDGE OF THE TRUTH."*

We should live with the realization that time is short and that we have important work to do. Be ready to meet Christ any time, even today, yet plan your course of service as though he may not return for many years. Pray, "without ceasing" for those you love and those God puts on your heart to pray for.

THE CROSS

August 7, 1916

The Christian cross is a representation of the instrument of the crucifixion of Jesus Christ, and is the best known symbol of Christianity. It is also a symbol of victory.

Movies of King Arthur and the Crusades show crosses on their garments, shields flags etc. These, of course, are movies, not reality, so we assume through history books that during that period, crosses were used as such.

"The Crusades was one of the most important events of the period, consisting in a series of religious Crusades in which Christians fought to retake Palestine from the Seljuk Turks. The Crusades impacted all levels of society in the High Middle Ages, from the kings and emperors who themselves led the Crusades, to the lowest peasants." (Taken from Remembering the Templars, Wikibooks on line.)

We, as Christians today, identify with our Lord Jesus Christ through the cross. There is nothing in which this identification is realized more than in prayer, the idea of prayer being perfect and complete oneness with God.

There are songs too numerous to mention concerning the cross. The simple cross represents Jesus' final victory over sin, which allows our salvation. Hallelujah!

In my own personal journey I was raised Catholic, using the crucifix as a religious symbol. My parents displayed such crosses all over the house. Although my family is not Spanish, it is an old Spanish custom to hang a cross over the bed to keep evil away, and we had crosses over our beds. Today, now being a Pentecostal, we have a cross with the Lord's prayer etched on it hanging over our front door and I wear a cross around my neck. I also have crosses on my Army uniform and

Vietnam Veteran Brotherhood vest identifying me as their Chaplain. I wear crosses on all my sport coats and suits too, as I am so proud to be a Christian and so thankful for what Christ did for us on the cross!

Funny story: At work one day, a customer was not happy. This man was a Hasidic Jew, which is a sub-group within Ultra-Orthodox Judaism and noted for it's religious conservatism and social seclusion. He was wearing their traditional garments--a black hat, prayer shawl and having a long beard and curls on each side of his head, all of which identify Hasidics. This customer was engaged in a heated discussion with one of my sales associates, yelling at the associate and pointing a finger into his chest. I looked up hearing him demand, "who and where is your boss!?" My associate, only too happy to pass on this irate customer, pointed to me. I was not far away and this customer then ran toward me, with his index finger pointing like a weapon. As he approached, he looked at my Chaplains cross on my lapel. His eyes got a scared look, he backed up and ran out of the store.

The power of the CROSS, Amen,

Thank you Jesus.

MIKEY'S MIRACLE

As Chaplain for the Vietnam Veterans Brotherhood (organization), one of my worst fears is the phone call I received one New Year's Day. One of our Brothers was in a motorcycle accident. We are all in our 60's-70's and all Vietnam Vets, and very close. The initial report was bad. He did not have his helmet on. The SUV in front of him stopped short and he flew forward into the back of the truck, bounced back down onto his bike, then hit the pavement. The diagnosis after X-rays and examination by the hospital doctors was Mikey had both legs broken, both hips broken, broken back, broken thumbs and a concussion. He has a preexisting condition of a deteriorating hip inoperable due to his weak heart, and he was on crutches or in a wheel chair gradually getting worse. They would not operate as he could die on the table. Now he was facing at least five surgeries!

I know you're wondering why in the world was Mikey riding a bike in the condition he was in. Well, we are Vietnam Vets. Nothing keeps us down!

I was upset as my wife and I entered his room. He was bruised and swollen with tubes coming out of everywhere. He was a mess. I had asked God, prior to the visit, to help me as I understood this was a battle. Mikey knew his situation. Looking at death from one surgery was one thing, but five surgeries was a sure disaster. My first prayer for him was for him to accept Jesus Christ as Lord and Savior. We quoted Romans 10:9, "*that if you confess with your mouth that Jesus is Lord and believe in your heart that God raised Him from the dead, you will be saved.*" Next I anointed him with oil as it says in James 5:14-16. My wife, Janet and I asked God to heal Mikey, praying in Jesus' name and believing God's word.

Due to the meds Mikey was on for his heart, the doctors needed to wait to do the surgeries. This gave me the opportunity to get the prayer request out to hundreds, possibly thousands of intercessors. The VIP team (Veterans Intercessory Prayer) which I had established in 1997 is a team of 60 members in 16 states around the country. We are Veterans praying in one accord, many whom are pastors who forward these prayer requests to their prayer teams. It is a mighty chain of mountain movers!

I felt a sense of peace as we left the hospital. Later, we went to a friend's house for a New Year's Day football game party where everyone there were Christians and we all prayed for Mikey.

Two days later we received an update that his first surgery went well! Praise the Lord! That was to correct the hip that was bad before the accident. He then had to go through extensive rehab, but with a positive prognosis. This was truly a MIRACLE healing and we give our Lord all the glory!!

CHARLES' ANGELS

One Sunday evening, a few years ago, I received a phone call from my daughter's mother-in-law, Marie, out in Oregon, who was very upset. Her son, my son-in-law, Charles, was working on his Ford Bronco when the jack popped out and the car rolled over him! As we were speaking, he was being taken away in an ambulance. First report was grim--chest, back, head and shoulder injuries. He was having trouble breathing and was in shock. Marie knew about my prayer ministry. I had also asked her to keep me informed of whatever was going on out there, as we are 3000 miles apart in SW Florida.

As soon as I finished with Marie's call, my wife and I prayed. I then went on my computer and put out an emergency prayer request to the VIP Team first, then to all other prayer warriors. As mentioned earlier in this book, the VIP Team is the Veterans Intercessory Prayer Team and has 60 members in 16 states, many who are pastors having their church prayer teams. One of the new members in linked to missions work in India and he has 2000 intercessors on his team. So, there were thousands of people now praying for Charles.

The second report was much better than the first. Charles was now stable except for the back injury. Test results were still pending. I was able to speak with him and as I prayed for his healing, he was very receptive. He told me he was not in any pain. I reminded him I pray for him and his family daily. I then asked him if he realized he could have been killed. He replied that he did realize that and said there were angels with him when the accident happened. He believed they saved him from being killed when that truck rolled over him.

Psalm 91:11, ***"For He, God, shall give His angels charge over you, to keep you in all your ways."*** This psalm has many of His promises. 91:1, ***"He that stays in the secret place of the most High shall abide*** *under the shadow of the Almighty."* This is the best way to dial 911 for an emergency!

How many angels do we need? Father God will supply us according to our needs.

That following Wednesday Charles was told he would need surgery on his back. Screws would be inserted to prevent any future problems. His surgery was scheduled for the next day. I spoke with him and asked him if he believed in God and he said he did. I then asked him to pray with me Romans 10:9, *"I confess with my mouth that Jesus is Lord and I believe in my heart that God raised Him from the dead....I am saved."* This is called the sinners prayer or a simple guarantee of salvation. Healing and salvation go hand in hand.

SAVING SLIM

As Chaplain for the Vietnam Brotherhood "B" Company, one of my duties is hospital visitation. Over the years I have been faithful visiting many and praying for their recovery.

Slim was in and out of the hospital several times. He had breathing problems related to cigarette smoking, and, as a result, had to always have oxygen with him. For as long as I knew him, he kept getting worse and his condition more serious.

Finally, I received a call that Slim was being sent to Hospice and late on one Thursday night his wife said he was asking for me. He did not know Jesus as his Lord and Savior.

Both myself and two other Christian Vietnam Veteran brothers had been ministering to him for a long time. That Friday morning, enroute to Hospice I took a wrong turn and almost got lost. This the enemy trying to block my getting there. His wife had said Slim was in and out of consciousness. I was praying I would have time to pray with him. As I entered his room it appeared he had already passed-- the man in the bed did not look like the Slim I knew. I asked the nurse if that was him in room 305. She checked and said yes it was. My heart sank. Then another nurse advised me Slim was in room 306. Praise God!

Entering room 306 I found Slim awake and a nurse was giving him breakfast. He recognized me and we talked. He knew he was terminal. I asked him if he would accept Jesus Christ as his Lord and Savior and he said yes. I asked him if he believe God raised Jesus from the dead and he said yes again. He also confirmed he was sorry for his sins. I quoted Romans 10:9-10, *"If you confess with your mouth that Jesus is Lord, and shall believe in your heart that God raised Him from the dead, you shall be saved. For with the heart man believes unto righteousness and with the mouth confession is made unto salvation."*

I told him all the angels in heaven stop to rejoice when someone accepts Jesus as Lord and Savior and is saved. I told Slim now heaven awaits him, and literally breathed a sigh of relief. I asked him if he was in pain and acknowledged he was so I anointed him with oil and prayed God would release him from the pain and give him comfort. I knew in my spirit there was a good chance God would very soon take him home and all pain would then disappear.

I then started to leave but somehow felt compelled to stay, so I sat with Slim for over an hour, praying silently as he had fallen asleep. A nurse then told me she had to provide breathing therapy so I needed to leave. I left him a Psalm 91 card and the hope of glory.

The next day, I got a call from his wife. He was sent home. Praise the Lord! Two weeks later he went home to glory. His wife said he told her he saw angels all around him.

Thank you Father God in Jesus name for SAVING SLIM!

PRAISE REPORTS

Before we moved to Florida, my wife and I took a trip down there to see about buying a home. We were living in New Jersey at the time and used Atlantic City Airport. It was very busy and crowded as we checked in. I had placed my bible on top of my carryon bag and was involved with getting our boarding passes. When I looked down, I realized the bible was gone. Someone had just stolen it. They most likely thought it was a lap top or I pad as it was in a leather case. I'm not sure what they thought, but they stole it.

This made me very upset as it was a special gift from my wife and had so many other notes, papers, and prayer lists in it. My wife and I immediately prayed for it's return and we prayed for the thief that stole it, then gave the situation to God. We were at peace because we knew God was in control.

About two weeks after we had returned home I got a letter in the mail. It was from a woman in Cape Coral, Florida who was claiming she had found my bible in a shopping cart at Walmart. My name and address were written on the inside cover so she was able to locate me. She gave me her phone number and asked me to call her, which I did. I was so delighted that she had contacted me! We then arranged for her to mail the bible back to me and I did tell her I would cover all expenses.

From some of the documents in the bible she learned I was a Minister. She shared with me that she was a Jehovah's Witness, and she had issues with the way my bible spoke about Jesus. I listened, silently praying for God to help me with this. I did not want to anger her---I wanted my bible back! After some time and conversation, we agreed on an amount for postage and I mailed a check the next day.

My wife and I continued to pray for this situation. We were not sure if she would mail the bible back, but in a few days, it came. Praise the Lord! Thank you, Jesus! The bible was in good shape but she had inserted a bunch of Jehovah Witness tracts and my small vile of anointing oil was gone. I had hung it on the zipper of the case. I have no idea why she would want that, or if it was already gone when she found the bible. My wife and I are not even sure she actually found it as she said, or she, or someone she knew, had been the one who stole it, but we decided to continue to pray for her. She did tell me had read several chapters so I believe some seeds were planted. The rest is up to God. Jeremiah 29:11, *"For I know the plans I have for you, declares the Lord, plans to prosper you and not to harm you, plans to give hope and a future."*

One of my students once asked, "Why are there so many denominations?" The answer is simple: because there are so many different opinions and ways of interpretation. We just need to trust God that He knows where and when to place you on your journey in Christ.

LET GO AND LET GOD

Today I let God take charge of this life of mine.

Now in the dark corners of my soul, His light is beginning to shine.

All of the cares and worries that I have carried for so long,

He has lifted them from my shoulders and filled my heart with song.

Problems that were overwhelming suddenly seem very small,

And come what may, starting today, by HIS grace and power, I can handle it all!

*If you are troubled, LET **GO AND LET GOD** take charge of your life for you and however dark life's shadows seem, His light will come shining through.*

Author: anonymous

POSTSCRIPT

I assumed I was finished with this book. God gave me a bit more, however. As I am in prayer looking for anyway to inspire my readers to pray, God gave me this:

Isaiah 64:7, *And there is none that call upon Thy Name that stirred up himself to take hold of Thee for Thou hast hid His face from us because of our iniquities."*

From the Hebrew (Chazag) "How to Pray:"

"To fasten upon, seize, be strong, courageous, obstinate, catch, cleave to, be constant, continue, force, lay hold on, maintain, play the man, wax mightily, prevail, retain, be urgent, wax strong. All these meanings can be understood in connection with prayer. If one would stir himself up in this manner, refusing to be denied, and if he would appropriate every benefit of promises and covenants with God, which have been freely and abundantly given to men--ALL men, then such a person would experience answers to prayer for body, soul and spirit for both himself and others."

Most essential thing in prayer:

"From the Hebrew (uwr), to open the eyes to awake. This is the most essential in the prayer life. One must stir himself up to pray and lay hold of God. The person who does will be blessed of the Lord. No man rises to God without effort. If one fails in this he sinks into sin and spiritual deadness which will take him to the lowest hell. The idea here is that of making an effort to rouse one's self when oppressed by a spirit of heavy slumber and extreme drowsiness."

This is Old Testament.

Written to the nation of Israel who had sunk into a spiritual stupor:

Isaiah is a miniature bible having 66 chapters corresponding to the 66 books of the bible, 39 chapters in the first section and the 39 books of the Old Testament. The second section has 27 chapters corresponding with the 27 books in the New Testament.

Chapter 64 is at the end of the New Testament chapters.

My prayer is that this book has inspired you:

DO NOT BE STINGY WITH YOUR PRAYERS!!

God bless you!

ABOUT THE AUTHOR

My husband, Tom Conti is an ordained Minister of the Gospel of Our Lord Jesus Christ, prayer counselor, Chaplain, teacher and intercessor. Although retired, he is engaged daily with being about the Father's business, led by the Holy Spirit. He is a runner and does about six 5k's a year.

Tom and I spearhead the Ministry, "Feed My Sheep" under the First Assembly of God, with our team we feed about 50 to 60 homeless weekly. Tom also leads the V.I.P. Ministry, which has about 50 Veterans praying in 16 states. We distribute food, clothing, and goodie bags to the homeless as well as prayer and the Gospel. John 21:16 Jesus asked Peter, "Do you love Me?" Peter replied, "Lord You know all things; You know that I love you." Then Jesus Said, "Feed My Sheep."

As Chaplain for the "Vietnam Brotherhood", he is blessed to pray for his Vietnam brothers and attend many veteran events.

Tom teaches basic prayer 101 and Bible history to the men at Teen Challenge. He is a Pastor and prayer counselor to help them get through the one-year program.

Tom served in Vietnam 1966 to 1967 Army First Infantry Division. He received numerous commendations for outstanding service. He also wrote a book, "MY CROSS TO BEAR" which is his personal experience "IN COUNTRY" and other helpful information for Veterans.

"Don't be Stings with your Prayers" has been in the works for about five years. The purpose of this book is to encourage everyone to pray daily and read the Bible.

Tom and I live in Cape Coral, Florida we have been married for 37 years. He has two daughters and three grandchildren. We have two yellow Labrador Retrievers and one goes running with him.

Both Tom and I thank God for His provision, health and protection as we are in a spiritual war against the enemy.

Pray for our Ministries and us we hope this book blesses you.

Here is a copy of the cover of Tom's first book, *My Cross to Bear*, about his year in Vietnam.

CPSIA information can be obtained
at www.ICGtesting.com
Printed in the USA
FFHW021848170619
53015569-58647FF